W9-AEP-874

Three Contemporary Novelists

Garland Reference Library of the Humanities (Vol. 52)

Three Contemporary Novelists :

*An Annotated Bibliography of Works
by and about*
JOHN HAWKES, JOSEPH HELLER,
and THOMAS PYNCHON

Robert M. Scotto

Garland Publishing, Inc., New York & London

1977

*PS
379
S 396*

*10/1978
am Lit*

Copyright © 1977
by Robert M. Scotto

All Rights Reserved

Library of Congress Cataloging in Publication Data

Scotto, Robert M   1942-
  Three contemporary novelists.

  (Garland reference library of the humanities ; v. 52)
    1. American fiction--20th century--Bibliography.
2. Hawkes, John, 1925-   --Bibliography. 3. Heller,
Joseph--Bibliography. 4. Pynchon, Thomas--Bibliography.
I. Title.
Z1231.F4S4 [PS379]   016.813'5'4   75-42889
ISBN 0-8240-9948-6

Printed in the United States of America

For Ruth Z. Temple,
   who has always known,
and for Joseph,
   who will

Contents

CONTENTS

Preface

Several principles are followed throughout the bibliography:

1. The novels (Section I) are listed chronologically. All other items are entered alphabetically. Only American editions of the novels are cited.

2. The citation of reviews for each novel is limited, for convenience, to ten. Several publications, as noted in the text, list more.

3. Important reviews are noted by an asterisk (*); these are annotated in Section V.

4. Only essays on the three figures covered, or significant critical statements that make mention of them, are annotated. Books such as *Catch-22*, for instance, appear in some fashion in any discussion of contemporary fiction, but the mere mention of the title does not signify inclusion here.

5. Dissertations (Section VI), stories, poems, and plays (Section II) are not annotated unless there is a specific need.

I would like to thank all those who helped me on this project, especially the scholars throughout the country who submitted their manuscripts, sometimes before publication, and often at their own expense. John Hawkes and Joseph Heller provided assistance and encouragement. Carol Hryciw, Hawkes' official bibliographer, will soon be publishing her bibliography for Scarecrow Press, and she cooperated graciously.

Introduction

I

John Hawkes, Joseph Heller, and Thomas Pynchon are among the more important writers of our age, their novels as different one from the other as the complex environment that spawned them, and as galvanizing. Although the twentieth century has seen many great novelists, and even more great novels, seldom have there been as many unique *voices* as there are in America today, writers who are forging revelations, who are proving fiction our most representative and most accomplished art form. Not since the earlier years of this century—in England, when Joyce and Woolf, Forster and Ford, Lawrence and Conrad, among others, and in America, during the twenties and thirties, when Hemingway, Faulkner, Fitzgerald, West, and Dos Passos were working simultaneously—has long prose fiction been so alive and so well, so filled with a sense of experiment, and yet so finely attuned to the disparate discord of its age. Surely, at a time when fiction has become such a powerful force within our culture, Hawkes, Heller, and Pynchon, each speaking in his own way, have more than secured their reputations; they each have become what we may call "contemporary classics," revered by the literary establishment and the academies, if not by the general public.

Of the three, Heller is the most difficult to classify because his two novels are so different, though this does not mean that he is any more or less important. Hawkes has become, along with Vladimir Nabokov most especially, our greatest lyric voice, our purest and most suggestive creator of visions. Pynchon is clearly our epic consciousness, the encyclopedic satirist of the age, working, most notably like William Gaddis, with the large tapestry superimposed upon the historical setting. Hawkes, like Virginia Woolf, does not write novels embedded in the quotidian, but rather evokes verbal universes peopled by characters who lie outside the mainstream, acute, sensitive, sensibilities whose reality is interior and subjective. His product is perfect books, tightly conceived, flawlessly executed, stylistically innovative. Pynchon, like the Joyce of *Ulysses*, is working with large chunks of space and time, with epic metaphor. His "facts" are, for the most part, historically valid, for he is attempting to forge a new *mythos*, a new set of lenses through which to focus on such recalcitrant materials, and to subsume enormous complexities within a satiric vision of contemporary man. The result is a variety of characters and caricatures, modes of narration and narrative styles. His ambitious books include more than it is conceivable to imagine a novel can hold, but hold they do, splendid monuments to an age wherein fiction may be the only product made by man that can reverse the "progress" that has finally begun to run in the opposite direction.

Catch-22, Heller's first novel, is, like Pynchon's *V.* or *Gravity's Rainbow*, a book filled with the manic inclusiveness of the later Joyce, with the same preferences for wit, satire, and allusion. *Something Happened*, however, is a very different vision indeed, an almost claustrophobic monologue whose virtue lies in its obsessive limitations, a book far closer, say, to Hawkes' later first-person narratives. Whereas Hawkes has developed technically away from his earlier, more surrealistically evoked nightmares in which character is difficult to hold on to, and Pynchon's vision has become more resonant while at the same time more rigidly controlled, Heller changed direction entirely, writing first a black humor classic and then, thirteen years after, limiting his scope to the ruminations and reflections of an "average" man as morbidly introspective and motionless as the awareness in the book it most clearly resembles, Beckett's *Watt*.

Altogether, by 1976, Hawkes has written seven novels, three novellas, and four plays; Heller, two novels and two plays; Pynchon, three novels. All three have published stories, while both Hawkes and Heller have written a few scattered essays and submitted to interviews; Pynchon, of course, has remained steadfastly out of the public eye, preferring an anonymity that has already become more than a small legend. The several critical distinctions with which they have been grouped—all three, for instance, are "black humorists," all three wrote powerful responses to World War II—hold them rather insecurely and yoke them together tenuously at best. Surely the comedy—or, to use the term Hawkes prefers and with which Pynchon would hardly disagree, the parody—in a recit like Travesty differs not only in degree but also in kind from Yossarian's ruminations and Slothrop's verbal felicities. At times labels are stretched so generously that they include more than they leave out, suggest more than they specify, and fail to discriminate among the works they treat as equals. The peculiar voices of Hawkes, Heller, and Pynchon will be considered in due time, but it is necessary to point out that critical opinion has clearly indicated to what extent they are respected among their contemporaries. Whatever we decide to call them—fabulists, absurdists, satirists—they are three of our most original writers.

Although World War II did not have the traumatic effect upon the West that the Great War did, it surely left its impact on our contemporary fiction as has no other historical event. The first novels of Hawkes (The Cannibal) and Heller (Catch-22) are clearly about the European conflict, and Pynchon's Gravity's Rainbow has been called literature's definitive statement about the holocaust. Echoes of the terrible consequences and ironies growing out of the war appear specifically in Hawkes' third and fourth novels (the Hencher scenes in The Lime Twig, the ominous background to Skipper's scenes with Cassandra in Second Skin) and within the panoply of Pynchon's entropic view of twentieth-century Western civilization in V. (the scene in which the now mechanical V is stripped by the boys in Malta, for instance). All three novelists are clearly moved by what has become the requisite tragic vision, but the ugliness, the sorrow, and the loss appear in very different guises. Hawkes' books are clearly about the interior life, the inner warpings that spring from childhood and dominate our civilization's undersides and underpinnings; he wants us to confront our guilt, our repressed fears. Heller's Catch-22 and Pynchon's three novels are about the outside that has crippled the contemporary romantic, the America brilliantly relocated within the militaristic (Catch-22) and historical (V.) detritus of the West, or even more cleverly superimposed upon the map of Europe (Gravity's Rainbow), the America that has become something less than the land of opportunity. Oedipa Maas (The Crying of Lot 49) and Yossarian are more sympathetically and fully drawn than most anti-persons, and their plight, as a result, has a greater immediacy to the reader than the parody and satire of the novels would promise at first:

they grow, as Slothrop inversely disintegrates, upon the sympathies. Bob Slocum, in *Something Happened*, needless to say, represents the product of a more clinical analysis of our age, and his impact is more negative: the only way to survive in this jungle, it is clearly implied, is to prevail.

Tracing the three careers should help the reader in two ways. First, the unique vision and craft of each writer will be further confirmed, especially since comparison is impossible; and second, the annotations, especially those of the critical responses to the novels, will be clearer if the contexts of the novelists' *oeuvres* are clearly delineated.

II

John Hawkes (born 1925)

The Cannibal (1949) grew slowly in significance as a first novel, waiting, like Hawkes' reputation, too long to be recognized for what it is: one of the most daring and ingenious works of experimental fiction written in America since the thirties. In retrospect, it appears to be not only one of the first important novels about World War II, but also one of the first important pieces of innovative fiction written in our generation by the man whom Leslie Fiedler once called "the least read novelist of substantial merit in the United States." When Hawkes decided to scramble the chronology, as Albert Guerard tells us, and reconstruct the point of view, he did more than make the novel difficult: he invested it with what has become a tone and an ambience peculiarly his own. Although he has created more difficult fictions (*Charivari, The Beetle Leg*), more fully controlled visions (*The Lime Twig, Death, Sleep & The Traveler*), and more dazzling linguistic microcosms (*Second Skin, The Blood Oranges*), *The Cannibal* is still, for better or worse, his most widely known "representative" performance. It is the first of his lyric evocations of the grotesque.

Most of the catalogues of "war" fiction do not include *The Cannibal*, in part because it triumphed slowly while other books made bigger splashes, but also because its surrealistic elements—a phrase Hawkes has a difficult time accepting as descriptive of his work—were so markedly different from the more "searing" and "epic" visions of conflict and apocalypse. Its correlations between history and fiction (the Archduke Ferdinand-Ernst episode, for instance) were too personally drawn, too interior for those who admired the explicitness of Remarque, Hemingway, Mailer, Shaw, or Jones. Before Hawkes, the marriage of ugliness and lyricism was not only rare, but actually a heresy within the great tradition. Few Joyces proved the exception. Today, of course, we have come to expect distortions of conventional fictional techniques, nightmare visions, fractured time, poetic place. Perhaps the "neglected" Hawkes may have had an impact in spite of his narrow audience.

The Cannibal is what Guerard, who has been Hawkes' herald from 1948, when he wrote the novel's preface, would call "anti-realist," though others might prefer the terms black humor, parody, or visionary. All apply because Hawkes' styles subsume rather than exclude opposites. Many times in the course of the novel certain scenes appear to extol both the themes and the styles in powerful epiphanies, but two that linger with the reader most vividly are the mayhem at the asylum and the skinning of the fox.

As the title indicates, men are reduced to beasts by war and its consequences: ideology, historical necessity, political hysteria. When the asylum that is used by Hawkes both to locate and to characterize Spitzen-on-the-Dein erupts in a riot, a piece of magical prose transforms the monkeys—used in various experiments—into the symbolic victims of thirty years of combat:

> One of the monkeys seemed to have grown, and frozen, was sitting upright on the bodies of the smaller beasts, tail coiled about his neck, dead eyes staring out through the gates, through the light of early morning as dim and calm as the moon. "Dark is life, dark, dark is death," he suddenly screamed as the women charged across the snow.

The most horrible scene in *The Cannibal*, and the most widely celebrated, is the duke's "kill"—the son of Madame Snow—and the meal that follows. No one moment in all of contemporary fiction, perhaps, better serves as a test case for black humor, and no one incident better sums up the disgust of the sensitive writer when confronted with the bestial:

INTRODUCTION

The organs and mutilated pieces gathered up in the small black fox's jacket, he tied the ends together, used his cane as a staff, and trudged up the hill, his long Hapsburg legs working with excitement. Behind him he left a puddle of waste as if a cat had trapped a lost foraging crow. But the bones were not picked clean and a swarm of small cream-colored bugs trooped out from the ferns to settle over the kill.

That Zizendorf, the novel's first-person narrator, could not have been witness to these events—as a matter of fact, nearly half of the novel occurs beyond his perceptions, especially since he is so obsessed by his revenge against Leevey through his neo-Nazi movement—enhances their horror. Projected as they are beyond one point of view, they settle all too uncomfortably into a vision of death-in-life that we can feel in the viscera. Nightmare has seldom carried such conviction as truth.

Charivari (1950) is the first of Hawkes' exotic novellas, set, like *The Lime Twig*, in an unnamed but imagined England, and fraught, like *The Cannibal*, with distortions of time, space, and context. This is truly a remarkable piece of surrealistic writing. The subject is the unusual marriage of Henry and Emily, their incredible families, and, by means of bizarre time-present narratives, which are simultaneously flashbacks, their wedding and her violation, possibly engendering the child that they announce to their guests is on its way. The title is ironic: the "shivaree" is the mock bridal song delivered to honeymooners; Henry and Emily are scarcely novices, though they are victims, and the environment that spawns them is really the major force in the story, killing, as it does, both the child in the womb, if it ever was there in the first place, and Henry's love. As the "Expositor," Henry's sleep-antagonist, aptly describes · the experience of *Charivari*:

It happened in a dream. It happened in one of those dazzling dreams, a dream of your omnipotence, when you lost track of time, when you were caught and fooled by space, by a shadow of perfume.

Stephen Koch has called *The Beetle Leg* (1951) Hawkes' masterpiece, a "surrealistic western" that is the first of his parodies of fictional genres, and, perhaps, his most difficult and taxing work. It is as impossible to describe what happens in the novel as it is to locate its peculiar sources of appeal, or the rightness of its recreation of the modern West. Perhaps the best approach is to think of time in a different way, or to rethink our perception of time as it informs a work of fiction. If the hill of mud in which Mudge Lampson is buried moves "a beetle's leg each several anniversaries," the events that swirl around the dam occur dizzyingly in both past and present, and with great impact. According to the sheriff's preface (and the narrator later on), we are trapped in "a lawless country" for roughly the fourteen or so years he has been in control; the main funnel through which the scenes are conveyed is Luke, the younger brother of the man trapped in the "Great Slide."

Time really becomes event. As we follow Luke from his domestic scene with Ma, his older brother's wife, and Maverick, the Mandan Indian servant, we move imperceptibly back to older days. For instance, his encounter with the tourist Camper family is interspersed with the history of the town Clare and the dam project; Ma's reflections on her dead husband generate her recollection of their bizarre courtship; the fishing expedition elicits more memories from Ma and others from Cap Leech, who may be the Lampsons' father, as well as Luke's memory of an earlier outing during which he fished out a mysteriously emblematic baby. Behind all these actions buzz the motorcycle gang, the Red Devils, who are finally confronted by the members of the fishing party in a bloody climax, wherein the weapons are discharged "into the belly of the dam." If fiction has the power of creating infinitely rich and suggestive textures, then *The Beetle Leg* surely has to be considered one of the textbook cases in our literature.

Hawkes' next two published works, although they were written earlier, were novellas set in Italy, *The Owl* and *The Goose on the Grave* (1954). Of the two, *The Owl* is the simpler, though no less rich; *The Goose on the Grave* is more surreal, more reminiscent of *Charivari*. Il Gufo tells his own tale, a bleak and macabre story about how he, the hangman, finally brings a visitor to "justice," partly to impress the "fathers" of Sasso Fetore, partly to avenge his name and further establish his power over this primitive community. The effect is all in the telling, however, for the sparse narrative line sparkles with lyric prose and is dominated by atmosphere, by gloom. The real conflict lies not only between Il Gufo and the spectacular prisoner, who captures the imagination of the townsmen and their marriageable daughters, but also between the hangman and the people who both fear him enough to avoid him but loathe him enough not to provide him with a wife. According to his own account he triumphs at the end, but for Hawkes the triumph of the book is in its language, the effect of such a tale refracted through such an unusual set of lenses, and in the powerful moments of pure evocation, especially the scenes in which the real owl is described or the prisoner makes his daring flight from the castle.

The Goose on the Grave is more picaresque in structure than *The Owl*, and is told in the third person, although most of the events are perceived, however dimly, by the child Adeppi. War dominates "Castiglione's city," and the theme is the spiritual desolation that follows the destruction and the ravages; the method of narration is surreal, the landscape distorted by the boy's temperament, dreams, and superstitions. A series of masters strip away his faith, his naiveté, and probably his virginity, and at the end he is the prisoner of the sinister priest Dolce, who, like a fury hovering in the background, slowly reclaims the scattered fragments of the "year of dissolution." Adeppi, "one of Italy's covey of fragile doves," is caged, his will broken like the neck of the goose, his future prospects, like the earth, cold. Once again, it is Hawkes' masterly ability to create fresh places and atmospheres that are indescribable precisely because they are so inseparable from the context they are drawn within; with *Charivari, The Goose on the Grave* is as close as any American work yet to the pure lyric novel.

The Lime Twig (1961) is Hawkes' parody of the detective thriller, his evocation of the lawless underside of society—the only time he has done this, although he has, especially in the later novels, dealt with characters who were technically criminals—and his imaginative recreation of an England he had never seen. It is probably his most admired novel, the one most often singled out as his masterpiece, praised by Flannery O'Connor, the writer Hawkes himself most admired at the time it was written. Like *Charivari* it is a book about British classes, about impotence, about an oppressive environment; unlike the earlier novella, *The Lime Twig* works, with a few notable exceptions, not surrealistically but through vividly evoked scenes and images. It is a novel written by a craftsman at the height of his powers.

After the initial chapter, in which Hencher introduces the reader to London, his lodgings, and his past in the first person, *The Lime Twig* deals with, in brief, the kidnapping of the racehorse Rock Castle by some thugs and the results accruing from their attempt to run him in the Golden Bowl at Aldington. Michael Banks, as soon as he is included in the cabal, emerges as the major character, and the only tragic one, especially after Hencher's gruesome death, and the remainder of the plot, with the exception of Sidney Slyter's bizarre racing column and a couple of isolated scenes, is realized mainly through his perception of the events in a third-person narrative.

Again, as in all of Hawkes' fiction, the reader remembers the vivid scene, the startling impression, the effective evocation of nightmare and gloom: when Rock Castle is being lowered into a van out of the hold of a ship on a pulley; when Hencher, who introduces Banks to Larry's gang, is battered to death by the horse; when Margaret, Banks' wife, is terrorized by her captors, who feel she will be insurance against her husband's possible betrayal; and when Banks, after realizing the grim realities of the situation, and after his dalliance with the temptress Sybilline fails to deaden his sense of guilt, sacrifices himself by throwing his body in front of the galloping Rock Castle during the home stretch of the race. Then there are the brilliantly realized thugs: Sparrow, Thick, Larry, their leader, all machismo and charisma. Helping to define the bleak landscape is the trenchant wit of Slyter, who both perceives and misses the plot afoot. Although the "Sidney Slyter Says" columns are slightly ahead of the action of the narrative, *The Lime Twig*, for all its resonances and challenges, is really the first novel of Hawkes' in which the chronology is roughly consecutive and the time commensurate with clocks and calendars. Although no less an accomplishment, it does represent a different tack. As it happens, the four novels that Hawkes has written since *The Lime Twig* are all first-person narratives, like the Hencher chapter, and all are parodies of literary genres and lyric evocations of eros, thanatos, or both.

It would be easy to group his latest books for convenience' sake as a tetrology, or, since *Travesty* was written after most of the essays on Hawkes' recent fiction, a trilogy plus one. They have certain shared preoccupations, their lyricism betrays a clear resemblance, and the narrators are, if not similar, then surely similarly obsessed. However, *Second Skin* (1964) also marks a change in direction for Hawkes, because for slightly more than a decade of his career he has explored the possibilities of first-person narrative and exorcised certain demon images (the lighthouse, for instance, in *Second Skin*, or the ship in *Death, Sleep & The Traveler*).

Second Skin is the only one of his novels that is drawn from an existing earlier sketch, "The Nearest Cemetery." It is a parody that is, like *Death, Sleep & The Traveler*, too difficult to specify: Skipper's cross-country trek and his less than heroic actions in time past, for example, have no clear source, except perhaps the road novel of the fifties and sixties; if that is the case, the younger days of Skipper are a mock-apprenticeship story in which tragedy rather than illumination regularly results. The novel's second "skin" is the time-present sequences on the "wandering" isle, which are both idyllic and yet fraught with hints of impotence. These passages and chapters are the most lyrically written (see the very beginning and ending of the novel: "I will tell you in a few words who I am: lover of the hummingbird that darts to the flower beyond the rotted sill where my feet are propped; lover of the bright needlepoint and the bright stitching fingers of humorless old ladies bent to their sweet and infamous designs. . . . I am now fifty-nine years old and I knew I would be, and now there is the sun in the evening, the moon at dawn, the still voice. That's it. The sun in the evening, the moon at dawn. The still voice.") and the most paradoxical; they are, like Cyril's lyricism in *The Blood Oranges*, romantically Shakespearean, but at the same time almost Swiftian. Note how words undercut Skipper's posture of passive joy: "rotted," "propped," "stitching," "humorless," "infamous," "still"; the repetition of the reversed cycle of the day without apparent cognizance of its possible ironies; the ominous nature of "voice" in light of his daughter's earlier fate. *Second Skin* is an apology for the life of a lover, a father, a sailor, and an artificial inseminator who is, at heart, sterile. He celebrates in lilting prose what his very actions belie.

The novel's major tension, then, is generated by its two time sequences. In the past is failure and pathos: the brutal homosexual murder of his son-in-law Fernandez; the suicides of his father and his daughter, Cassandra, both of which he was unable to prevent;

the violation of his body on the seas by Tremlow; the frustrations
he meets at the hands of Red, Jomo, Bub, and Miranda on the
bleak north Atlantic island that serves as a foil to the later
paradise. Perhaps his only victory is in the bumping contest in the
high school auditorium, but even that is undercut by the attack of
the snow balls that follows. In the present is Sonny, once his black
servant, now his equal, Catalina Kate, and the expected baby,
whose father is undetermined. This eden is less than idyllic,
however, as the vile iguana atop Kate's back brilliantly attests. Like
his story, it is filled with unexplained darknesses: Skipper, who
attempts to make his "harmless and sanguine self" into "a man of
courage as well," instead reveals only that once the oilcloth (which
he calls a second skin) is stripped away, and his words carefully
parsed, there remains simply a sad old man sterilized by his past.

The Blood Oranges (1971) is Hawkes' most ambitious novel, his
respectful parody of Shakespearean romance and Ford Madox
Ford's The Good Soldier, his deepest, most penetrating
psychological study[It is probably the closest great book to that
greatest of all contemporary novels, perhaps, Nabokov's Lolita:
the lyrical confessions of a brilliant but uneven and slightly
distorted mind whose main focus of attention is sexual love that,
in the opening line, "weaves its own tapestry, spins its own golden
thread, with its own sweet breath breathes into being its
mysteries." Hawkes has been accused of writing a deliberately
derivative novel, or worse, by those who admired the more
"experimental" earlier works, of surrendering to something less
than the pure aesthetic impulse. But The Blood Oranges is neither
derivative nor simple; it is, rather, a novel whose resonances are
drawn from a somewhat brighter, though surely not cheery, set of
images, and a more self-contained narrative point of view.

The plot for the most part involves Cyril's "more than eighteen
years" of his "nearly perfect marriage" with Fiona, his affair with
Catherine, Hugh's wife, and its consequences: "Illyria," the
landscape in southern Europe that is both imagined and
reproduced, is disrupted. Hugh commits suicide, Catherine falls
into madness, Fiona leaves with her children. As in a
Shakespearean comedy, the tangled web of sets of star-crossed
lovers is resolved, although here not happily; as in Ford's brilliant
analysis of extramarital love, the consequences of setting loose
pent-up passions are tragic. It is a novel that, as its title promises,

INTRODUCTION

is filled with ripeness, with lustiness, with love, but with horror, and death, and decay as well:

The sun was setting, sinking to its predestined death, and to the four of us, or at least to me, that enormous smoldering sun lay on the horizon like a dissolving orange suffused with blood.

Again:

Quietly I smiled at the symmetry of orange sky, chunks of bloodied wood, oars that projected into nothing more than air, boat that still lay several yards from the vast tide that would float it into life, and yet would one day reduce it to nothing more than a few cracked wooden ribs half buried in sand.

If Hawkes' vision has become "sunnier," as some insist, and if his situations have become more "accessible," they still contain an undertow of nightmare, of parody.

The Blood Oranges is filled with memorable, emblematic scenes: the church that Fiona and Cyril visit before their lovers arrive in Illyria; the barn wherein the peasant-girl Roselka strips for Hugh's camera; the grape arbor wherein the cross-seductions fructify; the fort that yields an ominous chastity belt; the coffin housing the dead dog held aloft in a solemn funeral procession; the boat-launching festival; Hugh's hanging. Cyril, who thinks of himself as "virile," the singer of polygamous love, is ultimately victorious over the stiff and photographically literal Hugh, but the triumph is mostly symbolic, and Pyrrhic to boot. The novel may be read in several ways: as a struggle between different moral systems whose tension is heightened in a land stripped of recognizable moral frames of reference, or as a struggle within the "lover's" psyche between two warring impulses. Hugh may be a Conradian "you." The consequences are both delicious and deadly.

Death, Sleep & The Traveler (1974) is closer to pure parody than any of the earlier books—as is *Travesty* (1976). Hawkes' last two novels confirm several predictions about his career, although virtuoso performances like these are, of course, unpredictable. Many critics, especially Albert Guerard, indicated that Hawkes would eventually tell tales that were more clearly "narratives"; Hawkes himself said that he would concentrate more heavily on parody, less on irrealist structures. *Death . . .* is a complex work and a complex play on previous fictions: on Dostoevski, perhaps, on the psychological novel in general, on Conrad, on the confessional novel, on the overzealous first-person narrative both nakedly honest and carefully disguised. *Travesty* is a parody of the French *recit*, and the one that most obviously comes to mind is Camus' *The Fall*.

Death . . . is told by another of Hawkes' neurasthenic narrators. All of the vignettes, the longest of which is about ten pages long, alternate between the major events of Allert Vanderveenan's middle-aged, sexually obsessed life: the triangle on shipboard circling around Ariane and the wireless operator, Olaf; the triangle he left at home involving his wife, Ursula, who is leaving him in the novel's time present, and Peter, his dearest friend, a psychologist who is proprietor of Acres Wild; his Kafkaesque dreams replete with his, his wife's, and his friend's interpretations. Minor recitatives dominate the novel's verbal universe, echoing the title, adding resonance to the meditation: his pornographic photographs and photographic imagery (an interest apparently shared by many of his latest characters); Ariane's fishhook scar and hook imagery; water and sea imagery; his rash; blood images, fetal images, ship images, island images; patterns of cold and warm, colors; the eucalyptus tree; smoking and drinking; patterns of sanity, paranoia, schizophrenia; homosexuality; childhood; sleep. There are, too, the usual startling scenes: the octopus, the sexual perversions of the bats in their cage. Puns abound (the protagonist's first name, for instance: it sounds as if it could be a description of his awareness; it is, however, ironically, the Dutch equivalent of Alan: "harmony"). It is a rich, unsettling, atmospheric novel.

Travesty is the most claustrophobic of Hawkes' novels, a monologue delivered by the driver of an automobile to his two passengers. The nameless narrator is Hawkes' obsessive and obsessed lover, like Cyril an aesthetician of sorts, whose aesthetic centers on the ecstasy of total destruction, the "utter harmony between design and debris," "the essential integrity of our tableau of chaos." He plans to drive his daughter, his daughter's friend, who is also his wife's lover, and himself to certain death, all the while justifying his act and recollecting, though not in tranquillity, the "travesty" of his past—he may have run over a little girl with an automobile years earlier—and of his present. Insanity is a travesty of sanity, as monologue is of conversation, as death is of life, as sickness is of health, as murder is of love. As in *Death, Sleep & The Traveler*, Hawkes is parodying a diary of a madman and a note from underground, but in this shorter, swifter book, the reader is more tightly gripped by the hypnotic prose and the upcoming triple sacrifice to an inverted sense of order. Hawkes is in absolute command of the diseased lyricism, the anti-aesthetic, of the narrator.

I accelerated. I saw the tassel flying. The old poet's face was a mass of rage and his umbrella was raised threateningly above his head. I felt nothing, not so much as a hair against the fender, exactly as if the child had been one of tonight's rabbits. I did not turn around or even glance in the rear-view mirror. I merely accelerated and went my way.

I do not believe I struck that little girl. In retrospect it does not seem likely. And yet I will never know. Perhaps the privileged man is an even greater criminal than the poet. At any rate I shall never forget the face of the child.

At the end, true to his promise, it would appear, although we cannot know because events come to us through the first person, he accomplishes his end. When he says "there shall be no survivors," a macabre thrill is generated. The alternate world of Hawkes is now in full control.

III
Joseph Heller (born 1923)

Catch-22 (1961) became, within a short time after its publication, one of the most galvanizing pieces of fiction in contemporary America, highly regarded, as few books before it, both within and outside of the academies. History, of course, had a great deal to do with its popularity, if not its reputation. Heller began to write the novel in the fifties, a decade or so after World War II and a decade before Vietnam. Conceived purely as a satire, and deliberately updated to bring the reader closer to the realization that the same forces that controlled the world in the forties control it still (a sentiment shared by Pynchon), *Catch-22* evolved into a tract for our times when its country finally caught up with it. It incorporated both hindsight and prophecy within a dazzling image.

The novel's "relevance," however, has obscured many of its virtues. Like all great war fiction, *Catch-22* is about more than the conflict it depicts; very few pieces of contemporary literature have illustrated so profoundly that the enemy is within. The villains are not the Germans or the Japanese, or, by a leap of historical imagination, the Russians or the Chinese, they are the power brokers who gain from the war—like Pynchon's "they" and "elect"—the sadists who enjoy violence, and all "average" men everywhere who acquiesce and die. If the major concern of modern fiction is, as many believe, to describe the futility of the individual within an environment that frustrates goals and essences, then surely Yossarian, the militant "deserter," he who is intent on running, is one of our most representative "anti-heroes."

Like many experimental novels, wherein structure adjusts to changes inside the protagonists, *Catch-22* does not end where it began. In Joyce's *A Portrait of the Artist as a Young Man*, for instance, the growth of Dedalus toward recognition is reflected in the maturing prose; *Catch-22* darkens appreciably in tone to accommodate Yossarian's decreasing sense of humor: the comedy becomes less farcical, more hysterical; the intricate chronology straightens out; tragedy becomes human rather than statistical. In other words, *Catch-22* is one of those rare novels that discovers its final form as it proceeds, as Yossarian discovers what he must do in light of where he is.

The last quarter of the novel, therefore, is different in tone from the first three-quarters, less picaresque in structure, more serious in mood, for it more clearly depicts Yossarian's growing awareness of pathos. At the beginning of the book, for instance, the reader soon realizes that the chapter headings, with very few exceptions (the brilliant comic reversal of the American dream in "Major Major Major Major" is the most noteworthy), forecast *imprecisely* the contents that follow—one of the many non sequitur techniques used to heighten the absurd activities on Pianosa. But after Kid Sampson is gruesomely sliced by McWatt (who kills himself and the absent Doc Daneeka) in Chapter XXX, and the chronology finally stabilizes to reveal that it is winter, during which the novel ends, the chapter headings become more

INTRODUCTION

painfully precise, the novel's tone deepens in bitterness, and its humor almost completely disappears. Doc Daneeka (XXXI), that other ironic American success story, and Mudd (XXXII), the "dead man" in Yossarian's tent, are effectively "disappeared" by the established (Towser) and newly minted (Yo-Yo's roomies) military machine. The surreal irony turns into nightmare when both the real and the unreal are unsafe. Love is made to seem insane and un-American by the devil-tempter old man whose logic, like that of Milton's Satan, is worldly and inexorable (XXXIII); Thanksgiving, a uniquely American feast, becomes a painful holiday climaxed by the return of the soldier in white (XXXIV); Milo finally reveals his true intentions to Cathcart, and Nately and Dobbs kill each other as a result of his "militancy" (XXXV); the chaplain is ruthlessly interrogated (XXXVI), the now *General* Scheisskopf takes over as commanding officer (XXXVII), and Nately's whore, who attempts to kill Yossarian after he breaks the bad news about her protector, is "chased away" by the authorities (XXXVIII).

The last four chapters, however, are a crescendo of horror. "The Eternal City" (XXXIX) depicts humanity, in the time-honored seat of religion and history, as thoroughly diseased and metaphorically diabolic. "Catch-22" (XL) illustrates the elite's power symbolically through Colonels Cathcart and Korn, who offer Yossarian a way out of the net if he will become a showpiece for the system, and for M & M Enterprises, a plan foiled at least in part by fate, in the presence of a knife in the hand of Nately's whore. "Snowden" (XLI) is a brilliant dream-fugue in which Yossarian, upon the operating table, recalls for the last time the full horror of Snowden's death, and hears that Hungry Joe was absurdly smothered during the night by a cat. All prophecies come true on Pianosa, and life is at least as dangerous to the warriors away from the front as it is on the battlefield. Events reoccur and people reappear, always closer to disaster, the only exception being Milo Minderbinder, the American "dream" come true in an otherwise nightmarish universe. In the final chapter, "Yossarian" (XLII), a fitting title for the conclusion of this central intelligence novel, Yossarian justifies his desertion as the only sane act left after all other modes of activity have failed. *Catch-22* ends on a darkling plain, bleak, wintry, and funereal—like the desolate heath Lear wanders over in his madness and grief—on its night side, its central character threatened by death in a world more attentive to red tape than to genocide, a world wherein everyone was more "different together in daylight than they were alone in the dark." Catch-22, in its absurdity and its evil, is now in full control.

Because *Catch-22* is a novel of discovery, a view of what life is like in an absurd world, the clearly delineated deepening in tone is Heller's perfect closure for the book's unique rhythm. At first Yossarian, who is intelligent, sensitive, and self-sufficient, dodges and uses humor as an escape, sees in it an antidote for the pain (the manner in which he censors letters, for instance). Soon, however, the laughter becomes strident. Because of the huge cast of characters and the complex plot, Heller's ability to draw character, despite his own disclaimers, is too lightly passed over and Yossarian considered merely a *ficelle* upon which the allegory is hung. But since he actually *changes*, so, too, does the novel. As the puppets are controlled more rigidly (Scheisskopf, who is in total command at the end because he runs the Special Services— the S.S.!—would like to sink metal pegs into each man's thighbone, linking wrist to leg with copper wire so that the arms would hardly move during the parades) and the blood flows more freely, the humor turns "blacker."

The manner in which Heller employs description to evoke a change in mood comparable to a change in the central intelligence is reminiscent, as we have indicated earlier, of Joyce, whose novels are the first in our language wherein stylistic change is fully coextensive with levels of realization. Each time an incident is retold in *Catch-22*, it is retold from a different viewpoint; it never remains the same. The many and varied moments of awareness define each new revelation with a more somber truth. *Catch-22* does not come full circle but rises to another plane: we are wiser about our zany and tragic world, and certainly sorrier.

We are aware immediately of entering a different world in the opening pages of *Something Happened* (1974). If *Catch-22* has one flaw, as most of its critics are anxious to point out, it is in being too inclusive, too ambitious in scope, confusing or obscuring its finer attributes in myriad details and a kaleidoscopic style. *Something Happened*, Robert Slocum's interior monologue about his personal life and career, as introspective and confined a novel as it is possible to imagine, is a departure in kind as well as in degree: gone is the torturous chronology Heller believed was a necessary refraction through which the characters' helpless agony was communicated; gone is the large canvas, the action, even plot in the lyrical sense. Rather, *Something Happened* is the somewhat paranoid confession of a moderately successful, "average" businessman who is not so much the victim of bureaucratic evil as of psychological paralysis, at least until the novel's final chapter. It is neither emblematic nor allegorical, but one of the purest works of *literature* written within the last decade, untranslatable and unadaptable, a novel impossible to conceive of in cinematographic terms.

Slocum's mind is obsessive and enclosed; indeed, as his obsessions and his interests generate the very feel of *Something Happened*, his monotonous voice mesmerizes and, finally, overwhelms. There are, first of all, his syntactical tics ("Ha-ha," being "emphatic"); there are the long set pieces of dialogue introduced by extended meditation and footnoted by his commentary; then there are the elaborate, complex parentheses—some several pages long—that both interrupt his reflections as well as punctuate them. What are his concerns? As Heller himself has said, "psychological survival" and "intimate combat." He is insecure and guilt-ridden; his mother's dying words, "You're no good," haunt him like a self-fulfilling prophecy. At the office he fears the bitter rivalries involved in making it up the corporate ladder ("I don't like closed doors, sick friends, bad news"). Green, his boss, he hates; Kagle, his immediate superior, he wants to unseat and ultimately does; he is afraid of the three-minute speech he must make at a convention, but finally pulls it off splendidly. Like Chaplain Tappman in *Catch-22* he imagines catastrophes with remarkable clarity, and his meditations are filled with prophetic, ugly dreams. At home he is the intimidator, the fury of the family; although he may get frustrated in suburban Connecticut, he is never a victim of "the willies" as he is in his New York office. His wife's theoretical infidelity, his daughter's pubescent scorn, his favorite son's insecurity, concretized in his inability to handle money, and his younger son, whom he no longer thinks of as human because of his imbecility, form the heart of his malaise, as most of the chapter headings indicate ("My wife is unhappy," "My daughter's unhappy," "My little boy is having difficulties," "My boy has stopped talking to me"). But there are other, more private obsessions still: his affair with Penny—indeed, his sexual liaisons in general—and his teen-age failure to make it with Virginia during his first office job; his neglect of his mother in a home after his father's early death; and many more. As the novel progresses, or fails to progress for nearly five hundred pages, Slocum becomes more genuinely evil or, at best, morally neutral, before his ironic success story is completed. As Heller said in the Plimpton interview: "I told several people while I was writing the book that Slocum was possibly the most contemptible character in literature. Before I was finished, I began feeling sorry for him." What a different protagonist from Yossarian, a sign of sanity, even if a bit feeble and manic, in an otherwise insane world. In *Something Happened*, one of the most unlikable products of our civilization is, at the end, in control. There is no message here, only, as Kurt Vonnegut pointed out in his review, "a depressingly ordinary fact."

Slocum's narrative monologue, therefore, is dominated by two interrelated themes: his self-loathing and stasis internally and the entropy of America in the twentieth century outside. This is how he describes his life:

I float like algae in a colony of green scum, while my wife and I grow old, my daughter grows older and more dissatisfied with herself and with me . . . and my little boy grows up tortured and puzzled, uncertain who, beside himself, he is supposed to be . . . or which of the many dangers he pictures are real and which are merely hideous and fantastic daydreams.

The ellipses in this passage indicate that Slocum has engaged in a long parenthesis. It actually takes two pages to complete this thought. Again Slocum muses:

I have had to stand still for the longest time now, it seems, for nearly all of my life. Nearly every time I search back I come upon myself standing still inside some memory, sculpted there, or lying flattened as though by strokes from the brush of an illustrator or in transparent blue or purple chemical stains on the glass slide of a microscope or on the single frame of a strip of colored motion picture film. Even when the film moves, I am able to view the action only in arrested moments on single frames. And yet I must have moved from where I was to where I've come, even while standing still.

INTRODUCTION

The world outside, while Slocum has drifted into stasis, is quietly sinking, like a pathetic fallacy, into deeper pits and doldrums: "More and more things seem to be slipping into a state of dissolution, and soon there will be nothing left." Again: "Dirty movies have gotten better, I'm told. Smut and weaponry are two areas in which we've improved. The world is winding down." Or, just before the novel's climax: "I feel locked inside a hopeless struggle."

Out of the tension between the two themes comes the resolution, and the title takes on further significance and a more terrible irony. For most of the book little has been happening, and Slocum, except in his remembrance of things past, has been going nowhere. His son, however, his favorite thing in the world, and the closest object he can be said to feel compassion for, dies. We are led to believe that it is murder, even if not consciously premeditated, for in the act of taking the boy into his arms after an automobile accident in a shopping center, Slocum literally squeezes life out of the fragile form. The official cause of death is listed as "asphyxiation." Something has finally happened.

Perhaps because he has exorcised at last the demon that has held him bound tenuously to life through sympathy, perhaps because he has quite literally nothing to lose, Slocum begins to "take command." His victory, however, though very tangible, is morally bankrupt, for there can be no doubt that his apathy has been translated into meanness, into coldness. He is, like the colors, not men, who work in his office ("Green," "Gray," "White," "Brown") a success story, not a human being.

Everybody is impressed with how bravely I've been able to move into Kagle's position and carry on with the work of organizing the convention. No one understands that carrying on bravely was the easiest thing to do.

The irony comes as much from Heller as Slocum; the narrator is simply negotiating the facts. This is progress, upward mobility, self-realization. In our world pathos is always this close. To borrow the final warning in the novel that Heller enjoyed reading while he was writing *Something Happened*, *Watt*, another profoundly simple and mercilessly comic vision: no symbols where none intended.

IV

Thomas Pynchon (born 1937)

V. (1963) is more than an awesome first novel. It is, without doubt, one of the finest tours de force in modern English, a structure without precedent written by a novice who is nonetheless a master of many styles. Part of its difficulty is the confusion it leaves in the reader about the author's strategy: why are so many difficult puzzles left unsolved and plot threads unresolved while others are clarified almost too carefully? Why the many and daring shifts in narrative point of view? Why the profound, precise research? Are we being entertained, taught, or manipulated? As Pynchon's career has since confirmed, probably all of the above.

V. is not really *about* any one thing; it is, in Professor Mendelson's word, Pynchon's first "encyclopedic" attempt to subsume contemporaneity's multiplicities and paradoxes, and to erect a design in spite of the chaos. Two main narrative threads meet in New York and, at the close, in Malta, the novel's "apocheir," which drew Stencil and Profane like "a clenched fist around a yo-yo string." The novel's time present is late 1955-1956, mainly in New York; its times past are, in their chronological order rather than their order in the book: 1898, Alexandria; 1899, Florence; 1904, South Africa; 1913, Paris; 1919, Malta; 1922, South Africa; 1939, Malta. Valletta, the novel's most dominant geographical "V.," is the scene of the climax of both stories: 1919 is the date of Stencil Sr.'s death, 1939 of the dismemberment of V., and 1956 of the book's now. The two men who occupy roughly the center stage of the two story lines are Benny Profane, the super yo-yo, the "schlimihl" for whom life is little more than a series of sensual highs—and who professes not to have "learned a goddam thing" from his experiences—and Herbert Stencil, Jr., "he who searches for V.," the man who gathers all of the historical incidents into a theory of personality that may not be correct, and uncovers what appears to be an international cabal of awesome power, which may not exist.

Seldom has a writer been able to slip in and out of so many narrative focuses and speak through so many different personae, and in only a few other instances has this facility appeared so early in a career. Read as entertainment, *V.* is dazzling; the vivid descriptive scenes—like the suck hour, the dismantling of the mechanical V., the alligator hunt, Hopl's seige party—are counterpointed against the more sedate historical ruminations of Stencil; from raunchy dialogue in New York to carefully re-created moments in the past, the novel is, though not as variegated as *Gravity's Rainbow*, a bravura exercise in writing. Like the mysterious, blinding white light that appears to several characters at crucial moments in the book, the effect of Pynchon's orchestration of scenes is devastating. Although *V.* is not without faults, and surely not without excesses, its virtues constantly prevail.

One example of its dazzling ingenuity is the two sequences that make up chapters three and four, ironically two of the three sections from *V.* published in excerpt. Three, "In which Stencil, a quick change artist, does eight impersonations" (published first as "Under the Rose"), is a complex introduction to the novel's historical story line; here we encounter the first clues that Stencil has accumulated concerning the enigmatic V. in Alexandria, 1898. We meet, from eight distinctly different points of view, Victoria Wren and the first cast of characters that launches her odyssey through some of the major crises of the twentieth century. The variations in style are truly impressive: Aïeul, "cafe waiter and amateur libertine," whose narrative is descriptive and matter-of-fact; Yusef, the "factotum" and "anarchist," who attempts to fathom the mysterious foreigners, though without great success; Maxwell Rowley-Bugge, the penniless "peregrine" who describes a conversation at Fink's dominated by V.; Waldetar, the train conductor who overhears the ominous conversation between Porpentine and Bongo-Shaftsbury on a trip into "the green triangle" of Cairo during which one of the novel's most famous and sinister lines is spoken: "'Humanity is something to destroy'"; Gebrail, the Arab phaeton driver, who bears Goodfellow to his seduction of V. and notes that import of the Fashoda Crisis, which dominates the chapter, may be likened to his horse's ass; Girgis, the burglar who overhears the plotters talking, in a scene filled with comedy, while hiding in a tree; Hanne, the barmaid, who contracts a triangular stain, like a V, on her arm—one of the many revelatory and prophetic moments in the novel; and, finally, an omniscient voice who describes the murder of Porpentine by Bongo-Shaftsbury.

INTRODUCTION

Four, "In which Esther gets a nose job," is a delightful scientific tour de force of a kind that has become one of Pynchon's trademarks. The Maxwell's demon and amok spray-can episodes in *Lot 49*, the many long excursuses in *Gravity's Rainbow* like the legend of Byron the Bulb, the "psychodontia" passage in Eigenvalue's office in *V.*—all are equally persuasive examples of the peculiar humor that seems hyperbolic precisely because it is photographically real. Pynchon's "science" is factual and dynamic, a medium through which he exposes foolishness, like the classical satirist, in its own terms; if science has become our century's divinity, he intimates, then look at what it has wrought. As Schoenmaker ("beauty-forger"!) re-does Esther's Jewish nose, she falls in love with her ravisher. Each step of the operation is described meticulously—the "undermining," the "shortening"— and each gesture emblematically records Esther's seduction, including the surgeon's mock-heroic serenade to the new her at the conclusion of the festivities. The result is pure Pynchon:

Have I told you, fella
She's got the sweetest columella
And a septum that's swept 'em all on their ass;
Each casual chondrectomy
Meant only a big fat check to me
Till I sawed this osteoclastible lass:
(Refrain)

The Crying of Lot 49 (1966) was mistaken at first as a smaller *V.*, a lesser vision, more streamlined, perhaps, but not as resonant. The years have done much to establish this slim classic as something greater than the short book Pynchon wrote between his two epics, however, and it is almost superfluous to add today that in addition to being his most "accessible" novel, *Lot 49* is slowly becoming his most widely read one. Perhaps the fact that Oedipa Maas is his most human character has something to do with it, or that the Tristero is his most concretely realized conspiracy, less awesome, certainly, than any "elect," but cleverly and cynically evoked. Pynchon's "science" is graphically present, too, in hilarious good form. Finally, the enormous range of styles that Pynchon first exhibited in *V.* are here more maturely implemented. *Lot 49*, rather than being a stay of continuance, represents an important development.

At the core of all of Pynchon's fiction is a paradoxical statement about the nature and extent of our free will. On the one hand, the cabals that permeate the underside of New York and European civilization (*V.*), California (*Lot 49*), and the entire west (*Gravity's Rainbow*) are apparently in total control, feeding us just enough information for us to think we have a hand in shaping our destinies. On the other hand, there are frequent moments of illumination occurring to the "we," the victims, into the nature and composition of the "elect," the power grids of civilization. Pynchon's characters vacillate rapidly between insight and ignorance, both reinforcing their paranoia and producing a tension composed in roughly equal parts of broad comedy and touching pathos. Profane and Stencil are rather ineffectual at ferreting out the truth while Slothrop gradually loses his battle to hold on to his identity against his powerful enemies. Oedipa, however, is quite different. She is not only more inquisitive than Profane, more intelligent than Stencil, and more variegated than Slothrop, she is an enormously dynamic, likable, and interesting person in the bargain. Moreover, at the end of *Lot 49*, as she awaits the "crying" of the stamp collection she has traced assiduously to San Narciso, not far from where she began, "trying to guess which one was her target, her enemy, perhaps her proof," she comes closer than any other of Pynchon's protagonists to breaking through to the secret, to translating the mystery underpinning the quotidian she has refused to accept at its face value.

Pynchon evokes southern California with devastating accuracy, and with loving satire, its variety and contradictions aptly mirrored in its different styles. There is the breezy ("One summer afternoon Mrs. Oedipa Maas came home from a Tupperware party whose hostess had put perhaps too much kirsch in the fondue to find that she, Oedipa, had been named executor, or she supposed executrix, of the estate of one Pierce Inverarity, a California real estate mogul who had once lost two million dollars in his spare time but still had assets numerous and tangled enough to make the job of sorting it all out more than honorary."), the irreverent ("today she came through the bead-curtained entrance around bar 4 of the Fort Wayne Settecento Ensemble's variorum recording of the Vivaldi Kazoo Concerto, Boyd Beaver, soloist"), the ironically reflective ("Such a captive maiden, having plenty of time to think, soon realizes that her tower, its height and architecture, are like her ego only incidental: that what really keeps her where she is is magic, anonymous and malignant, visited on her from outside and for no reason at all."), the ominous ("Smog hung all round the horizon, the sun on the bright beige countryside was painful; she and the Chevy seemed parked at the centre [sic] of an odd, religious instant."), the recreated historical (the tale of the Peter Pinguid Society, *The Courier's Tragedy* of Richard Wharfinger, the documents of the Thurn and Taxis, the Tristero, the WASTE system, the Inamorati Anonymous), the scientific (Nefastis's explanation of entropy and Maxwell's demon), the lyric ("The saint whose water can light lamps, the clairvoyant whose lapse in recall is the breath of God, the true paranoid for whom all is organized in spheres joyful or threatening about the central pulse of himself, the dreamer whose puns probe ancient fetid shafts and tunnels of truth all act in the same special relevance to the word, or whatever it is the word is there, buffering, to protect us from. The act of metaphor then was a thrust at truth and a lie, depending where you were: inside, safe, or outside, lost."), and literally dozens more. *The Crying of Lot 49* may be one of our slimmest classics, yet many richnesses are enclosed in so short a text. For those who like the ebullience and scope of the other Pynchon, *Lot 49* may end too soon, but it is difficult to deny that it is his most finely honed and most carefully tuned vision of doomsday, even if it is not his fullest.

Gravity's Rainbow (1973) is the epic of the seventies, the most exhaustive and exhausting novel to appear in several decades. It is not impossible to find a dissenting voice in the otherwise overwhelming tide of praise that greeted its publication, but it is difficult to find one who does not temper his reservations with respect, even awe. If such a novel is flawed—and what book this ambitious cannot be to most people at most times?—then so be it. Few masterpieces hold us line by line, and few novels written since World War II have so clear a claim to the honor.

Gravity's Rainbow is a bigger book than *V.*, yet more tightly focused. The results are both more rewarding and more taxing to the reader: although there are bravura moments unequaled in our fiction (the attack of the giant Adenoid, the Disgusting English Candy Drill, the Rocketman and Pig-hero episodes, the Story of Byron the Bulb, to name but a few), there is an almost claustrophobic density—although the scope is European at least—that V.'s repeated opening-out relieved. It is a darker, more technical, and far more resonant experience, yet it is, nonetheless, a book whose rereadings are both justified and rewarding.

The protagonist—and emblematic victim—is Tyrone Slothrop, the irresistible, irrepressible but naive rich boy-schlimihl who, whether under loose scrutiny in London or on the Riviera, or hunted after he escapes into the post-war German war zone, is the creature of experiment to a behaviorist cartel of such immense power that only the Byron the Bulbs of the world are capable of avoiding its penalties for deviancy. He somehow comes into contact with all of the other major characters and forces in the book: with Pointsman, the Pavlovian who controls The White Visitation; with Mexico, who sympathizes with the "we" against his fellow pure scientists who are running the tail end of the war for the "elect"; with Tchitcherine, the Russian officer who is looking for his black half-brother; with Enzian, the South African rocket expert, who is attempting to reconstruct Captain Blicero's Rocket 00000; the list is extensive, variegated. Certain characters from V. appear earlier in their careers (Pig Bodine, here "Seaman"; Kurt Mondaugen), and the hint in the earlier novel that the first decade or so of the twentieth century in South Africa was a prophecy of the holocaust is, of course, more than amply illustrated.

Pynchon's erudition and exotic research have never been more fully displayed. The operations of the huge corporations (General Electric, Siemens, Shell, Standard Oil, I. G. Farben) that run the world are carefully delineated; the theories of Max Weber, Pavlov, Kekulé, Einstein, and Whitehead are exploited; reinterpretations of Wagner, Mann, Rilke, among others, abound; references to Calvinism, Manichean extremes, Herero rituals, as well as exotic journeys like Tchitcherine's to the Kirghiz light, or the Schwarzkommandos' to the true north, or Slothrop's through the Boston sewer system, run throughout the novel. Beneath all of the images or allusions, however, in fact generating them, is the technology of the rocket, one of the most awesome symbols in modern literature. *Gravity's Rainbow* may well be the most successful work of fiction with such a clearly scientific underpinning, just as it is one of the most noteworthy works of "high" literature employing all of the trappings of kitsch and pop cultures as reverently and as resonantly as the classics.

INTRODUCTION

History for Pynchon is neurosis; progress induces paranoia; entropy has infected not only the universe of energy but the accessibility of knowledge, the utility of communication, as well. Slothrop wanders through and across the "Zone" of newly occupied Germany, but he is actually journeying through much more: the map of America superimposed upon Middle Europe, his destiny as well as ours. As he ceases to be "any sort of integral creature any more," and is reduced to "fragments" and "personae" of his "original scattering," we are witness to more than his "disappearing," as Yossarian would have called it; the grids of energy controlled by the elect have accomplished what the emissaries of The White Visitation could not. No one escapes Big Brother. The threat, moreover, is still upon us. At the end of *Gravity's Rainbow* the Rocket is poised above "the roof of this old theatre," both a movie house somewhere in the neighborhood, we can assume, and the very same "theatre" that described the evacuation of bombed-out London in the novel's first lines: "It is too late. The Evacuation still proceeds, but it's all theatre." The same living dead, the preterite who were killed by weapons they could not hear and see, are today following "the bouncing ball" on the screen; the lights then disappeared ("No lights anywhere"), the lights are now dimming fast ("at this dark and silent frame") as the brennschluss reaches the "last delta-t." Everybody sings the centuries-old hymn of poor Tyrone's ancestor, an ominous warning about "the last poor Pret'rite one" haunted by "the Riders" in the "crippled Zone." "And in the darkening and awful expanse of screen something has kept on, a film we have not learned to see, it is now a closeup of the face, a face we all know"— and the show begins again. We have been recycled (or reincarnated, duplicated, propagated) without essential change; earth's gravity (Pynchon's deliberate pun) still exercises its hold. *Gravity's Rainbow*, in one sense, is one of the gravest assessments of the human predicament in a century noted for its wastelands. It is, however, redeemed by its ambivalence toward science (what is destructive can also be harnessed creatively), and society (the preterite outnumber the elect, and victory, though difficult, is not impossible), and Pynchon's irrepressible and irreverent humor. The apocalyptical has never had so attractive a gift wrap.

V

Concluding remarks tend to draw arguments together and confirm patterns, but since our purpose throughout has been to provide a framework within which challenging fiction might be confronted, analogies will not be sought. It may be observed in passing that Heller's *Catch-22* could have had a conceivable impact on the young Pynchon writing *V.*, mainly in verbal echoes and gallows humor, or that the career of Hawkes could have inspired those of Heller and Pynchon, but observations that are so obvious tend to be unprovable. Hawkes has more or less admitted that his precursors were Nathanael West, Djuna Barnes, Flannery O'Connor, and a few poets; Heller has pointed to Celine, among others, as an inspiration for *Catch-22*; although Pynchon's intricate puzzles are virtually untraceable, it cannot be totally wrong to point to William Gaddis's *The Recognitions* as the one contemporary novel, more than any other, that may have helped shape his sensibilities. One clear assertion may be made about allusions in the novels of all three: they are nearly always parodic. Although critics have argued that certain books have directly inspired Hawkes (Ford's *The Good Soldier* and *The Blood Oranges*) or Heller (*Journey to the End of the Night* and *Catch-22*), or Pynchon (Adams's *The Education of Henry Adams* and *V.*), the ultimate value of their novels clearly lies in their ubiquity—in their ability to parody conventions rather than adopt them—and in their satiric humor. When commentators point out that what our age needs desperately is a great satirist, they need go no farther than the nearest bookstore.

Three Contemporary Novelists

I
The Novels of Hawkes, Heller, and Pynchon

i. Hawkes

1   The Cannibal. Norfolk, Conn.: New Directions, 1949.
     New York: New Directions Paperbook,
     1962.

     REVIEWED:
1a   Kirkus Reviews, 15 January 1950, p. 38.
1b   New Yorker, 28 January 1950, p. 85.
1c   Time, 55 (6 February 1950), 90, 92.
1d   Christian Science Monitor, 18 February 1950, p. 4.
1e   Ben Ray Redman. Saturday Review, 11 March 1950,
     pp. 16-17.
1f   John Roger. Harvard Advocate, 133 (27 March 1950),
     20.
1g   Alexander Klein. New Republic, 27 March 1950, p. 20.
1h   Wallace Marshfield. Commentary, 9 (April, 1950),
     392.
1i   Robert Gorham Davis. Partisan Review, 17 (Summer,
     1950), 522.
1j   Chicago Review, 4 (Winter, 1950), 44-45.

     REPRINTED:
1k   "Death of a Maiden." Wake, 6 (Spring, 1948), 85-96.
     "Love" chapter.

     This is Hawkes' first published piece of fiction,
     written while an undergraduate at Harvard during
     Albert Guerard's creative writing course.

1l   "Riot at an Institution." A New Directions Reader,
     eds. H. Carruth and J. Laughlin. New York:
     New Directions, 1964, pp. 136-142. "Leader"
     chapter.

2   Charivari. New Directions 11 (1949), 365-436.

     REPRINTED:
2a   Lunar Landscapes. New York: New Directions, 1969,
     pp. 51-136.

3   The Beetle Leg. New York: New Directions, 1951.
     New York: New Directions Paperbook,
     1967.

1

REVIEWED:
3a   Robert Reynolds. New York Times Book Review, 30
      December 1951, p. 12.
3b   Newsweek, 38 (31 December 1951), 58-59.
3c   New Yorker, 12 January 1952, p. 82.
3d   William Pfaff. Commonweal, 25 January 1952, p. 407.
3e   Saturday Review, 9 February 1952, p. 35.
3f   Robert Phelps. New Republic, 18 February 1952, p.
      21.
3g   Henry Politzer. Commentary, 13 (May, 1952), 514.
3h   *Robert Creeley. New Mexico Quarterly, 22 (Summer,
      1952), 239-41.
3i   Curworth F. Flint. Sewanee Review, 60 (Autumn,
      1952), 713-14.
3j   Albert J. Guerard. Perspectives USA, 1 (Fall, 1952),
      168-72.

REPRINTED:
3k   "Sarcophagus of Mud." The Personal Voice: A Con-
      temporary Prose Reader, ed. Albert J. Guerard,
      et. al. Philadelphia: Lippincott, 1964, pp. 587-
      91. Section of Chapter 4.

4   The Goose on the Grave (with The Owl). New York: New
      Directions, 1954.

REVIEWED:
4a   Frederick Yeiser. Cincinnati Enquirer, 23 May 1954,
      p. 35.
4b   James L. Dickey. Houston Post, 5 June 1954, Sec.
      5, p. 4.
4c   Louisville Courier-Journal, 20 June 1954, Sec. 3,
      p. 9.
4d   Columbia Missourian, 1 July 1954, p. 4.
4e   Vivian Mercier. Commonweal, 2 July 1954, p. 323.
4f   Nation, 3 July 1954, p. 17.
4g   Jerome Stern. Saturday Review, 24 July 1954, pp.
      35-36.
4h   Mona Thurston. St. Louis Post-Dispatch, 17 August
      1954, p. 20.
4i   Patrick F. Quinn. Hudson Review, 7 (Autumn, 1954),
      464.
4j   Virginia Quarterly Review, 30 (Autumn, 1954), xcii.

REPRINTED:
4k   Lunar Landscapes. New York, New Directions, 1969.
      "The Owl," pp. 137-199, "The Goose on the Grave,"
      pp. 200-275.
4l   "The Courtier." New Directions 13 (1951), 236-45.
      Opening pages of "The Goose on the Grave."
4m   "The Lay Brothers." New Directions 14 (1953), 281-
      87. "The Confession" chapter of "The Goose on the
      Grave."

2

5   The Lime Twig. New York: New Directions, 1961.
                New York: New Directions Paperbook,
                1961.

        REVIEWED:
5a   New Yorker, 29 April 1961, p. 149.
5b   Ray B. West, Jr. New York Times Book Review, 14
                May 1961, p. 31.
5c   Albert J. Guerard. New York Herald Tribune Lively
                Arts, 25 June 1961, p. 32.
5d   Joan Didion. National Review, 15 July 1961, pp.
                21-22.
5e   F.W. Dupee. The Reporter, 20 July 1961, p. 56.
5f   Virginia Quarterly Review, 37 (Summer, 1961),
                lxxxii.
5g   Webster Schott. The Nation, 2 September 1961, pp.
                122-23.
5h   R. V. Cassill. New Leader, 30 October 1961, pp.
                27-28.
5i   Phoebe Adams. Atlantic, 208 (November, 1961), 192.
5j   *Claire Rosenfield. Minnesota Review, 2 (Winter,
                1962), 149-54.

        REPRINTED:
5k   "The Lodging House Fires." Audience, 7 (Spring,
                1960), 61-77. Section of "Hencher" chapter.
5l   "The Horse in London Flat." Accent, 20 (Winter,
                1960), 3-19. Section of Chapter 1.
5m   "Hencher." The Single Voice, ed. Jerome Charyn.
                New York: Collier, 1969, pp. 176-193. "Hencher"
                chapter.

6   Second Skin. New York: New Directions, 1964.
                New York: New Directions Paperbook, 1964.
                New York: Signet, 1965.

        REVIEWED: (** reprinted in Studies in Second Skin. ed.
                John Graham. See #77)
6a   **Erik Wensberg. Vogue, 1 January 1964, p. 22.
6b   **Christopher Ricks. New Statesman, 11 March 1966,
                pp. 339-40.
6c   Granville Hicks. Saturday Review, 28 March 1964,
                pp. 25-26.
6d   Stanley Edgar Hyman. New Leader, 30 March 1964,
                pp. 24-25.
6e   Robert Adams. New York Review of Books, 5 April
                1964, pp. 12-13.
6f   **Susan Sontag. New York Times Book Review, 5 April
                1964, p. 5.
6g   **Stanley Kaufman. New Republic, 6 June 1964, pp.
                19-20, 22.
6h   *Paul Levine. Hudson Review, 17 (Autumn, 1964),
                470-77.
6i   *David Madden. Kenyon Review, 26 (1964), 576-82.

6j   **Peter Brooks. Encounter, 26 (June, 1966), 68-72.

      REPRINTED:
6k   "Honeymoon Hideaway (circa 1944)." Texas Quarterly,
         6/2 (Summer, 1963), 20-32. Section of "Wax in
         the Lilies" chapter.
6l   "The Heart Demands Satisfaction." Vogue, 15 January
         1964, pp. 72-73, 75, 112. Section of "Wax in the
         Lilies" chapter.

7   Lunar Landscapes. New York: New Directions, 1969.
                        New York: New Directions Paperbook,
                                   1969.

      CONTAINS:
         "The Traveler," pp. 1-11.
         "The Grandmother," pp. 12-25.
         "A Little Bit of the Old Slap and Tickle," pp. 26-30.
         "Death of an Airman," pp. 31-37.
         "A Song Outside," pp. 38-42.
         "The Nearest Cemetery," pp. 43-50.
         Charivari, pp. 51-136.
         The Owl, pp. 137-99.
         The Goose on the Grave, pp. 200-75.

      REVIEWED:
7a   Publisher's Weekly, 27 January 1969, p. 90.
7b   Jib Fowles. New Leader, 12 May 1969, pp. 26-28.
7c   Eric Moon. Library Journal, 15 June 1969, p. 2486.
7d   Robert Scholes. New York Times Book Review, 13
         July 1969, pp. 4-5, 32.
7e   Tom Bishop. Saturday Review, 9 August 1969, p. 31.
7f   Virginia Quarterly Review, 45 (Autumn, 1969), cxxvii.
7g   Choice, 6 (November, 1969), 1222.
7h   William Heath. Kenyon Review, 32 (1970/71), 186-90.
7i   John Wain. New York Review of Books, 26 February
         1970, pp. 35-38.
7j   Clive Jordan. New Statesman, 1 May 1970, p. 634.

      REPRINTED:
7k   Charivari. New Directions 11 (1949), 365-436.
7l   "Death of an Airman." New Directions 12 (1950),
         261-66.
7m   The Goose on the Grave. New York: New Directions, 1954.
7n   The Owl. In The Goose on the Grave. New York: New
         Directions, 1954.
7o   "The Grandmother." New Directions 17 (1961), 51-64.
7p   "A Song Outside." San Francisco Review, 1/2 (June,
         1962), 4-9.
7q   "A Little Bit of the Old Slap and Tickle." The
         Noble Savage, 5 (October, 1962), 19-23; and
         Harvard Advocate, 104/2 (October, 1970), 7-8.
7r   "The Traveler." MSS, 1 (Winter, 1962), 166-75; and
         New Directions 18 (1964), 162-70.

4

7s   "The Nearest Cemetery." San Francisco Review Annual,
        1 (Fall, 1963), 178-185; and Studies in Second
        Skin, ed. John Graham, pp. 38-43; and Write and
        Rewrite, ed. John Kuehl, pp. 266-72.

        The short story which Hawkes admits is the original
        germ from which Second Skin grew. As analyzed by
        John Kuehl in Write and Rewrite, the "pervasive
        symbolism concerns death," and the setting, char-
        acters, and mode of narration, though "vague" as
        preliminary drafts tend to be, do look forward to
        the novel.

8   The Blood Oranges. New York: New Directions, 1971.
                            New York: New Directions Paper-
                                book, 1972.

        REVIEWED:
8a   *Charles Moran. Massachusetts Review, 12 (Autumn,
            1971), 840-45.
8b   Christopher Lehmann-Haupt. New York Times, 15 Sep-
            tember 1971, p. 45.
8c   Thomas McGuane. New York Times Book Review, 19
            September 1971, p. 1.
8d   Pearl K. Bell. New Leader, 4 October 1971, pp.
            17-18.
8e   Philip Kravitz. Village Voice, 14 October 1971, pp.
            27-28.
8f   Roger Sale. New York Review of Books, 21 October
            1971, pp. 3-4, 6.
8g   Ronald DeFeo. Saturday Review, 23 October 1971,
            pp. 92, 94.
8h   Gerald Weales. Hudson Review, 24 (Winter, 1971/72),
            716-30.
8i   New Republic, 27 November 1971, p. 29.
8j   Virginia Quarterly Review, 48 (Winter, 1972), xviii.

        REPRINTED:
8k   "From a Forthcoming Novel." Harvard Advocate 104/2
            (October, 1970), 5. Reprint pp. 16-17.
8l   "Burnt Orange." Dutton Review, 1 (1970), 137-50.
            Reprint pp. 58-72.
8m   "From The Blood Oranges." TriQuarterly, 20 (Winter,
            1971), 113-129. Selections from opening pages
            (15-16).
8n   "Swapping." Fiction, 1/1 (Spring, 1972), 21-22
            (unpaged). Selections from pp. 37-45.

9   Death, Sleep & The Traveler. New York: New Directions,
                                        1974.
                                      New York: New Directions
                                        Paperbook, 1975.

REVIEWED:

9a Calvin Bedient. New Republic, 20 April 1974, pp. 26-28.
9b David Bromwich. New York Times Book Review, 21 April 1974, pp. 5-6.
9c Richard Todd. Atlantic, May, 1975, p. 130.
9d Celia Betsky. Nation, 18 May 1974, pp. 630-31.
9e *Stephen Koch. Saturday Review, 1 June 1974, pp. 20-22.
9f Charles Nichol. National Review, 7 June 1974, pp. 659-60.
9g Rust Hills. Esquire, July, 1974, p. 21.
9h Philip Corwin. National Observer, 20 July 1974, p. 21.
9i *W. M. Frohock. Southwest Review, 59 (Summer, 1974), 330-32.
9j Michael Wood. New York Review of Books, 8 August 1974, pp. 40-41.

REPRINTED:

9k "The Ship." Fiction, 1/4 (May, 1973), 22-25. Selections from opening pages.
9l "In Dante's Forest." American Review, 20 (April, 1974), 60-70. Selection from pp. 116-127.
9m "The Animal Eros." Antaeus, 13/14 (Spring/Summer, 1974), 70-78. Selections from passim.

10 Travesty. New York: New Directions, 1976.

REVIEWED:

10a Publisher's Weekly, 16 February 1976, p. 80.
10b Dennis Pendleton. Library Journal, 15 March 1976, p. 834.
10c Robert F. Moss. Saturday Review, 20 March 1976, p. 25.
10d John V. Knapp. Chicago Sun-Times, 21 March 1976, p. 9.
10e Tony Tanner. New York Times Book Review, 28 March 1976, p. 23.
10f New Yorker, 19 April 1976, p. 134.
10g Charles Nicol. National Review, 30 April 1976, p. 461.
10h Thomas LeClair. New Republic, 8 May 1976, p. 26.
10i Kirkus Reviews, 1 June 1976, p. 24.
10j J.T. Gilboy. Best Sellers, 36 (June, 1976), 69.

REPRINTED:

10k "Dead Passion." Fiction, 4/1 (1975), 17-19. Selections from pp. 62-75.
10l "Design and Debris." TriQuarterly, 35 (Winter, 1976), 7-9. From pp. 76-79.

11   Catch-22. New York: Simon and Schuster, 1961.
            New York: Dell paperback, 1962.
            New York: Delta paperback, 1964.
            New York: Modern Library, 1966.
            New York: Simon and Schuster, 1969. Large
              type edition.
            New York: Clarion paperback, 1969. Large
              type edition.
            New York: Delta paperback, 1973. Critical
              edition.

     REVIEWED: (Note: only reviews reprinted in either
            Critical Essays on Catch-22, ed. Nagel,
            or A Catch-22 Casebook, eds. Kiley and
            McDonald [see nos. 81 and 82] are listed.
            Joseph Weixlmann's bibliography has the
            fullest notation of reviews.)
11a   Granville Hicks. Saturday Review, 14 October 1961,
            p. 32.
11b   Richard Stern. New York Times Book Review, 22 Octo-
            ber 1961, p. 50.
11c   Milton R. Bass. Berkshire Eagle, 31 October 1961,
            p. 6
11d   Nelson Algren. Nation, 4 November 1961, pp. 357-58.
11e   Robert Brustein. New Republic, 13 November 1961,
            pp. 11-13.
11f   John J. Murray. Best Sellers, 15 November 1961,
            p. 345.
11g   Richard Starnes. Washington Daily News, 1 March
            1962, p. 25.
11h   Shimon Wincelberg. New Leader, 14 May 1962, pp.
            26-27.
11i   Newsweek, 1 October 1962, pp. 82-83.
11j   *Daedalus, 92 (Winter, 1963), 155-165.

     REPRINTED:
11k   "Catch-18." New World Writing, 7 (New York, 1955),
            204-214.

     The original version of chapter one ("The Texan")
     of Catch-22. It is interesting to note how much
     description and dialogue Heller cut when he re-
     vised the novel, the winnowing method being no-
     where more visible than in this instance.

11l   Black Humor, ed. Bruce Jay Friedman. New York:
            Bantam, 1965, pp. 23-40. "Milo" chapter, XXIV.

11m   "Love, Dad." Playboy, December, 1969, pp. 181-82,

348. Reprinted in A Catch-22 Casebook, ed. Kiley
and McDonald, pp. 309-16, and A Critical Edition
of Catch-22, ed. Scotto, pp. 447-55.

The chapter which Heller cut from the published
version of the novel is interesting because of the
light it sheds, perhaps too clearly for Heller's
original purpose, on one of the central preoccupations of Catch-22. Nately's father reveals himself,
through a series of letters giving advice to his
naive son, as an emblem of that segment of society
which not only gained from the war, but probably
precipitated the conflict into the bargain.

11n   The Single Voice, ed. Jerome Charyn. New York:
      Collier, 1969, pp. 125-36. "Snowden" chapter, XLI.

12   Something Happened. New York: Knopf, 1974.
                    New York: Ballantine paperback,
                    1975.
      REVIEWED:
12a   Kurt Vonnegut, Jr. New York Times Book Review,
      6 October 1974, pp. 1-2.
12b   Walter Clemons. Newsweek, 14 October 1974, p. 116.
12c   Melvin Maddocks. Time, 14 October 1974, p. 87.
12d   John Thompson. New York Review of Books, 17 October
      1974, pp. 24-26.
12e   John W. Aldredge. Saturday Review/World, 19 October
      1974, pp. 18-21.
12f   Calvin Bedient. Nation, 19 October 1974, p. 377.
12g   Edward Grossman. Commentary, 58 (November, 1974),
      78.
12h   L. E. Sissman. New Yorker, 25 November 1974, p. 193.
12i   Nelson Algren. Critic, 33 (December, 1974), 90-91.
12j   Wilfred Sheed. New York Times Book Review, 2 Febru-
      ary 1975, p. 2.

      REPRINTED:
12k   "Something Happened." Esquire, September, 1966, pp.
      136-41.

      The original version of the opening pages of the
      novel.

                    iii. Pynchon

13   V. Philadelphia: Lippincott, 1963.
      New York: Bantam paperback, 1964.
      New York: Modern Library, 1966.

      REVIEWED:
13a   Time, 15 March 1963, p. 106.

13b	Stanley Edgar Hyman. New Leader, 18 March 1963, pp. 22-23.
13c	Ihab Hassan. Saturday Review, 23 March 1963, p. 44.
13d	Newsweek, 1 April 1963, p. 82.
13e	Arthur R. Gold. New York Herald Tribune Books, 21 April 1963, p. 21.
13f	George Plimpton. New York Times Book Review, 21 April 1963, p. 5.
13g	Whitney Balliet. New Yorker, 15 June 1963, pp. 113-14.
13h	Irving Feldman. Commentary, 36 (September, 1963), 258-60.
13i	Christopher Ricks. New Statesman, 11 October 1963, p. 492.
13j	*Frederick J. Hoffman. Critique, 6 (Winter, 1963/64), 174-77.

REPRINTED:

13k	"Under the Rose." The Noble Savage, 3 (1961), 223-51. Original version of Chapter 3, "In Which Stencil, a quick-change artist, does eight impersonations."
13l	Black Humor, ed. Bruce Jay Friedman. New York: Bantam, 1965, pp. 1-16. Chapter 4, "In which Esther gets a nose job."
13m	The Single Voice, ed. Jerome Charyn. New York: Collier, 1969, pp. 137-58. Chapter 14, "V. in love."

14   The Crying of Lot 49. Philadelphia: Lippincott, 1966.
                        New York: Bantam paperback, 1967.

REVIEWED:

14a	Granville Hicks. Saturday Review, 30 April 1966, p. 27.
14b	Richard Poirier. New York Times Book Review, 1 May 1966, p. 5.
14c	Newsweek, 2 May 1966, p. 104.
14d	Time, 6 May 1966, p. 109.
14e	J. R. Lindroth. America, 14 May 1966, p. 700.
14f	Remington Rose. New Republic, 14 May 1966, p. 39.
14g	Oscar Handlin. Atlantic, May, 1966, p. 127.
14h	Roger Shattuck. New York Review of Books, 23 June 1966, pp. 22-24.
14i	Eric Wensberg. Commonweal, 8 July 1966, pp. 446-48.
14j	Stanley Trachtenberg. Yale Review, 56 (October, 1966), 133.

REPRINTED:

14k	"The World (This One), The Flesh (Mrs. Oedipa Maas), and the Testament of Pierce Inverarity." Esquire, December, 1965, pp. 170-73, 296, 298-303. Chapters 1 and 2.
14l	"The Shrink Flips." Cavalier, March, 1966, 32-33,

89-92. Section of Chapter 5.

X 15   Gravity's Rainbow. New York: Viking, 1973.
                             New York: Viking paperback, 1973.
                             New York: Bantam paperback, 1974.

          REVIEWED:
15a   Time, 5 March 1973, p. 74.
15b   Richard Locke. New York Times Book Review, 11 March
             1973, pp. 1-3.
15c   Newsweek, 19 March 1973, p. 23.
15d   Michael Wood. New York Review of Books, 22 March
             1973, pp. 22-23.
15e   *Richard Poirier. Saturday Review of the Arts, 1
             March, 1973), 59-64.
15f   W. T. Lhamon. New Republic, 14 April 1973, p. 24.
15g   E. Shorris. Harper's, June, 1973, pp. 78-80.
15h   Robert K. Morris. Nation, 16 July 1973, pp. 53-54.
15i   Philip Morrison. Scientific American, October, 1973,
             p. 131.
15j   William Pritchard. New Statesman, 16 November 1966,
             p. 734.

II
Uncollected Stories; Plays and Poems

i. Hawkes

Carol Hryciw, Hawkes' official bibliographer, has
been given access to his papers and unpublished manuscripts.
Her bibliography, to be published by the Scarecrow Press,
will contain much additional information, therefore.

16   Fiasco Hall. Cambridge: Harvard, 1943. Poems, private-
      ly printed.

17   The Innocent Party. New York: New Directions, 1966.
                New York: New Directions Paper-
                    book, 1967.
      Four Plays: The Innocent Party, The Wax Museum,
      The Undertaker, and The Question.

18   "Little Beatrice." Harvard Advocate, 130 (April,
      1947), 12. Poem.

19   "The Magic House of Christopher Smart." Harvard Advo-
      cate 130 (May, 1947), 14. Poem.

20   "The Universal Fears." American Review 16 (February,
      1973), 108-123. Story.

ii. Heller

There is a collection of Heller's working materials
for Catch-22, including letters, translations of the novel,
notes, stories, and other oddments, in the Special Collections Room at the Brandeis University Library.

21   "Bookies, Beware!" Esquire, May, 1947, 98 ff. Story.

22   "Castle of Snow." Atlantic, March, 1948, 52-55. Story.

23   Catch-22: A Dramatization. New York: Samuel French,
      1971. Acting version.
                New York: Delacorte, 1973.
                New York: Delta paperback,
                    1973.
      Library edition, with author's preface.

24   "Girl from Greenwich." Esquire, June, 1948, 40-41,
      142-43. Story.

25   "I Don't Love You Anymore." Story, September/October
      1945, pp. 40-44.

      In an issue devoted to stories "by or about men who
      saw service in the armed forces" appears "Lt."
      Joseph Heller's first story.

26   "MacAdam's Log." Gentlemen's Quarterly, December,
      1959, pp. 112, 166-76, 178. Story.

27   "A Man Named Flute." Atlantic, August, 1948, pp. 66-
      70. Story.

28   "Nothing To Be Done." Esquire, August, 1948, pp. 73,
      129-30. Story.

29   "World Full of Great Cities." Nelson Algren's Book
      of Lonely Monsters. New York: Bernard Gels, 1963,
      pp. 7-19.

      REPRINTED:
29a   Big City Stories, eds. Tom and Susan Cahill.
      New York: Bantam, 1971, pp. 15-25.

      This is the most widely read story of Heller's, and
      was written in 1949, when he was an undergraduate at
      New York University.

30   We Bombed in New Haven. New York: Delta, 1969.
                            New York: Dell paperback, 1970.

      Heller's widely produced play.

                          iii. Pynchon

31   "Entropy." Kenyon Review, 22/2 (Spring, 1960), 277-92.

      A very important statement in fictional form of one of
      Pynchon's most seminal themes.

32   "Low-Lands." New World Writing 16 (1960), 85-108.
      Story.

33   "Mortality and Mercy in Vienna." Epoch, 9/4 (Spring,
      1959), 195-213. Story.

34   "The Secret Integration." Saturday Evening Post, 19
      December 1964, pp. 36-37, 39, 42-44, 46-49, 51.
      Story.

35   "The Small Rain." Cornell Writer, March, 1959, pp.
      14-32/

      Pynchon's first published story, written while he
      was an undergraduate at Cornell. Nathan "Lardass"
      Levine, the protagonist, anticipates characters like
      Benny Profane and Pig Bodine of V. Matthew Winston
      (see his "The Quest for Pynchon") detects autobio-
      graphical elements in it.

Interviews; Critical and Biographical Materials

i. Hawkes

36   Enck, John. "John Hawkes: An Interview." <u>Wisconsin</u>
      <u>Studies in Contemporary Literature</u>, 6/2 (Summer,
      1964), 141-55.

      REPRINTED:
36a   <u>Studies in Second Skin</u>, ed. John Graham, pp. 23-31,
       in exerpt.

      An important interview in which Hawkes discusses, as
      he always does, with great candor, several ideas:
      innovation in fiction, especially the lack of an Amer-
      ican avant-garde, his favorite writers, the writer's
      detachment, comedy in his fiction, and writing about
      "fresh" worlds, landscapes and visions.

37   "Flannery O'Connor's Devil." <u>Sewanee Review</u>, 70 (Sum-
      mer, 1962), 395-407.

      REPRINTED:
37a   <u>Flannery O'Connor</u>, ed. Robert E. Reiter. St. Louis:
       <u>Herder</u>, n.d., pp. 25-37.

      Hawkes' discussion of a "comic" writer who is also a
      "serious" writer "in her moral pre-occupations, her
      poetic turn of mind and incredible uses of paradox."
      The "confluence" of O'Connor and Nathanael West upon
      Hawkes suggested to him "twin guffawing peals of
      thunder above a dread landscape quite ready for a new
      humor, new vision, new and more meaningful comic
      treatments of violence." He states: "if it appears
      that Flannery O'Connor is writing about the spirit
      (the absurdity of disbelief), while Nathanael West
      was writing about the dream (the powerful absurdity
      of sexual desire), at least I would say that the
      "pitch" of their comic fictions is very nearly the
      same."

38   "<u>The Floating Opera</u> and <u>Second Skin</u>." <u>Mosaic</u>, 8/1
      (1974), 17-28.

      John Hawkes discusses the relationship between his
      novel and the early novel of John Barth, and the
      relationship between the two novelists in general.

39   Graham, John. "John Hawkes on his Novels." Massa-
        chusetts Review, 7/3 (Summer, 1966), 449-61.

        REPRINTED:
39a   Studies in Second Skin, ed. John Graham. pp. 31-33,
        in exerpt.

        Hawkes discusses the "immediacy" of his fiction, the
        evolution of his work through Second Skin, and comedy,
        as he sees it, in his work and the work of those
        writers he admires. His remarks on the ending of The
        Lime Twig ("You could say, conceivably, that the
        ending of that novel is redemptive. I am very leery
        of saying that, however, because I am not a religious
        writer.") and on the comedy and first-person narrator
        in Second Skin are especially instructive.

40   Keyser, David and French, Ned. "Talks with John
        Hawkes." Harvard Advocate, 104/2 (October, 1970),
        6, 34-35.

        The interview with Keyser is largely the intervier's
        reflections, although Hawkes does admit that The
        Cannibal was written in nine months whereas The Lime
        Twig took "a very long time" to complete. French's
        speculations are speckled with Hawkes' reflections:
        that he would "just as soon write only middles" of
        novels, for instance, or that fiction "is the
        aesthetic and imaginative creation of moments, of
        situations." There are also some good observations
        on Hawkes' language.

41   Kuehl, John. "Interview," in John Hawkes and the Craft
        of Conflict, pp. 155-83.

        An important and lengthy interview in which Hawkes
        discusses: the iconoclastic intent of his fictions,
        his use of myths, his "death-ridden" fiction, his
        conception that "the highest forms of comedy may not
        produce laughter," the "picaresque" attitudes of his
        fiction, his respect for style ("everything depends
        on language"), and his sense of himself as a "surreal-
        ist" writer dealing with "comic absurdity."

42   "The Landscape of the Imagination," with George Mac-
        beth and others. Transcript of BBC broadcast, 2
        November 1966.

43   "Notes on Violence." Audience, 7 (Spring, 1970), 60.

        This brief essay is best summarized in the opening
        sentence: "Between the contemporary poem and experimen-
        tal novel there is not so much an alliance as merely
        the sharing of a birthmark: both come from the same

place and are equally disfigured from the start."

44   "Notes on The Wild Goose Chase." Massachusetts Review,
        3/4 (Summer, 1962), 784-88.

        REPRINTED:
44a   Studies in Second Skin, ed. John Graham, pp. 20-23.

        Hawkes discusses the relation of long fiction to
        poetry, especially in their creation of landscape,
        the pure creative impulse of Djuna Barnes, Flannery
        O'Connor and Nathanael West, and the necessary "de-
        tachment" of the writer from his work. With the kin-
        ship between poetry and "experimental" fiction "may
        be found the climate of the imaginative process."

45   "Notes on Writing a Novel." TriQuarterly, 30 (Spring,
        1974), 109-26.

        Hawkes discusses Second Skin as a novel which lends
        itself well to "the discussion of the fiction pro-
        cess." After outlining the genesis of the novel, he
        then turns to some of the visions which haunt him
        (the ocean liner, for instance, which he did use in
        Death, Sleep & The Traveler) as well as an analysis
        of the prose in his first novella, Charivari. He makes
        the following significant statement: "the association
        of the 'barely remembered woman,' who is idealized for
        her 'faint flush of youth,' with a vast violent world
        of death, sexlessness, and misogyny, is in fact the
        thematic center of all that I've written."

46   Scholes, Robert. "A Conversation on The Blood Oranges."
        Novel, 5/3 (Spring, 1972), 197-207.

        REPRINTED:
46a   The New Fiction, ed. Joe David Bellamy. University
        of Illinois Press, 1974, pp. 97-112.

        Hawkes discusses certain aspects of his novel: its
        "sexuality," Cyril and Hugh as "polar opposites, ver-
        sions of a single figure," the genesis of the novel
        in "a small vision, literally seen," the "visual"
        nature of his fiction, his attempt to "reveal the
        essential beauty of the ugly," and his "theory" that
        "fiction should achieve revenge for all the indignities
        of our childhood," and "be an act of rebellion against
        all the constraints of the conventional pedestrian
        mentality around us."

47   "The Voice of Edwin Honig." Voices, 174 (January/April,
        1971), 39-47.

        A critical tribute to the poet whom Hawkes has frequently cited as one of his exemplars.

48   "The Voice Project: An Idea for Innovation in the
      Teaching of Writing," in Writers as Teachers/
      Teachers as Writers, ed. Jonathan Baumbach. New
      York: Holt, 1970, pp. 89-144.

      Hawkes' description of his "intermediate" writing
      course, taught at Harvard and Brown, whose task was
      to "encourage the non-fiction writing student" to
      write "in a personal and identifiable prose, rather
      than in 'machine' or 'voiceless' prose." The author-
      ial "voice" is then explored, first by Hawkes'
      "theatre techniques" (pp. 93-103) and by the class-
      room experience of the "Voice Project," logged by
      Zeese Papenikolas (pp. 103-110). The rest of the
      piece is by Thomas Grissom, and is entitled "The
      Black Voice: Teaching at the College of San Matteo."

                        ii. Heller

49   Amos, Martin. "Joseph Heller in Conversation with
      Martin Amos." New Review, 2/20 (November, 1975),
      55-59.

      A discussion of Heller's work habits, the component
      of "madness" in both of his novels, the "psychological
      structure" and "accuracy" of his fiction, and the
      relevance of Something Happened, especially, to
      contemporary America and its morality.

50   Balch, Clayton L. "Yossarian to Cathcart and Return:
      A Personal Cross Country." A Catch-22 Casebook,
      eds. Kiley and McDonald, pp. 301-06.

      A personal essay about the relationship between
      Heller's depiction of the air war and the author's
      reminiscences.

51   Barnard, Ken. "Joseph Heller Tells How Catch-18 Be-
      came Catch-22 and Why He Was Afraid of Airplanes."
      Detroit News, 13 September 1970, pp. 19, 24, 27-28,
      30, 65.

      REPRINTED:
51a   A Catch-22 Casebook, eds. Kiley and McDonald, pp.
        294-301.

      An informal recollection of an interview in which
      Heller discussed his difficulties in writing Catch-22,
      its translation into film, and his work on the then
      unfinished Something Happened.

52   Braudy, Susan. "Laughing All The Way to Truth." New
      York Magazine, 14 October 1968, pp. 42-45.

      A brief interview centering on We Bombed in New Haven
      and concentrating mainly on biographical facts and
      quirks. An interesting passage discusses the genesis
      of the play.

53   "Catch-22 Revisited." Holiday, April, 1967, pp. 44-60,
      120, 141-42, 145.

      REPRINTED:
53a   A Catch-22 Casebook, ed. Kiley and McDonald, pp.
        317-332.

      A personal travelogue written by Heller after he had
      returned to Italy over twenty years after the war.

54   Gold, Dale. "Portrait of a Man Reading." Book World,
      20 July 1967, p. 2.

      A very brief interview.

55   Green, Gael. "Labor-saving Vices." Book Week, 6 Febru-
      ary 1966, p. 6.

      In response to an inquiry on procrastination among
      writers Heller replied briefly that the tape-recorder
      is his chiefest villain, followed by typing perfection.

56   Gross, Martin L. "Conversation with an Author." Book
      Digest, 3/5 (May, 1976), 14-15, 20-23.

      Heller discusses the novel he is presently writing
      (about "a fairly ambitious college professor from
      Coney Island...who becomes the first Jewish Secretary
      of State."), the implied themes of Something Happened
      ("Something bad had happened to the family."), its
      reception, and his evaluation of Catch-22 ("a complex
      and very dark book.").

57   Harte, Barbara, and Carolyn Riley. "Joseph Heller."
      Contemporary Authors: A Bio-Bibliographical Guide
      to Current Authors and Their Works. Detroit: Gale,
      1969, pp. 533-34.

      A brief sketch.

58   "Heller, Joseph." Current Biography, 34/1 (1973), 23-25.

      A brief biography.

59   "Heller, Joseph." Vogue, 1 January 1963, p. 112.

A brief biographical-critical sketch.

60   "How I Found James Bond, Etc." Holiday, June, 1967, pp. 123-25.

A brief account, laced with humor, of Heller's experiences with film.

61   "Irving is Everywhere." Show, April, 1967, pp. 104-05, 126-27.

A humorous account of the sale of the movie rights for Catch-22.

62   Krassner, Paul. "An Impolite Interview with Joseph Heller." The Realist, November, 1962, pp. 18-31.

REPRINTED:
62a   A Catch-22 Casebook, eds. Kiley and McDonald, pp. 273-93.
62b   A Critical Edition of Catch-22, ed. Scotto, pp. 456-78.

In the first, and perhaps still most significant, interview Heller discusses the initial reception of Catch-22 within its first year of publication, some of the books which influenced him, some of his intentions in Catch-22, and, finally, in a general way, the then contemporary scene. By far the most important pages deal with his explanation of theme and technique.

63   Lester, Elenore. "Playwright-in-Anguish." New York Times, 3 December 1967, pp. 1D, 19D.

During rehersal of We Bombed in New Haven at Yale, Heller admits that he doesn't like the theatre: "I think it's a very limited medium."

64   Mandel, George. "Dialogue with Joseph Heller." Penthouse, May, 1971, pp. 54-56, 59-60, 98.

A mainly personal interview, confined to Heller's opinions on contemporary events, and his reactions to Catch-22 and We Bombed in New Haven.

65   Merrill, Sam. Interview. Playboy, June, 1975, pp. 59-61, 64-66, 68, 70, 72-74, 76.

A long interview, introduced by a lengthy biographical sketch. The first part centers on the origins of the characters of Catch-22; it is followed by Heller's comments on politics, his early "New Yorker" stories, the origin of Something Happened, his personal interests, the present writers he admires (Updike, Nabokov,

Vidal), and other items.

66   "On Translating Catch-22 Into a Movie." A Catch-22
      Casebook, eds. Kiley and McDonald, pp. 346-62.

      An informal history of the making of the film, origi-
      nally delivered as a lecture, followed by a question
      and answer section. When he discusses the novel Heller
      says some interesting things about its structure, its
      manipulation of time, and its "literary" quality.

67   Philips, McCandlish. "Heller Pleased with 'Catch-22'
      Film." New York Times, 19 June 1970, p. 24.

      A brief interview in which Heller admits that he
      liked Mike Nichols' movie "as much for its infidelity
      to the book as for its faithfulness to it."

68   Plimpton, George. "The Craft of Fiction, LI: Joseph
      Heller." Paris Review, 15 (Winter, 1974), 126-47.

      A long and important interview in which Heller dis-
      cusses his methods of composition and his uses of
      fictional technique in both Catch-22 and Something
      Happened.

69   Plimpton, George. "How It Happened." New York Times
      Book Review, 6 October 1974, pp. 2-3, 30.

      A brief interview in which Heller explains the gene-
      sis of Something Happened and his method of "receiv-
      ing" first lines before the novels begin to take
      their shape.

70   Review of Evelyn Waugh's The End of the Battle. Nation,
      20 January 1962, pp. 62-63.

      An unfavorable reaction to the "serious" Waugh and
      his "dry and unimaginative"protagonist, Crouchback.
      "For someone who has never read Evelyn Waugh," he
      concludes, "this would be a poor place to begin. For
      many who always read him, this may, unfortunately,
      seem a good place to stop."

71   Sale, Richard. "An Interview in New York with Joseph
      Heller." Studies in the Novel, 4/1 (Spring, 1972,
      63-74.

      An interview during which Heller talks about the
      conscious literary nature of his work, its form and
      structure--"patterns of recurrence," "circular motion"
      --his use of dialogue, the novel Something Happened,
      which he was then finishing, and its affinity to the
      work of Samuel Beckett, the history of We Bombed in

New Haven, and his appraisal of Celine, Mann, Camus and Dostoevsky.

72   Shapiro, James. "Work in Progress: Joseph Heller, an Interview." Intellectual Digest, 2 (1971), 6-11.

An interview centering mainly on the genesis of Something Happened.

73   Shenker, Israel. "Joseph Heller Draws Dead Bead on the Politics of Gloom." New York Times, 10 September 1968, p. 49.

Mainly a personal interview conducted during rehearsal for the Broadway opening of We Bombed in New Haven.

74   "So They Say: Guest Editors Interview Six Creative People." Mademoiselle, August, 1963, pp. 234-37.

A brief, innocuous and sketchy interview in which Heller admits he had Faulkner's Absolom, Absolom in mind in order to capture "the feeling of simultaneous sweep" in Catch-22.

75   "Too Timid to Damn, Too Stingy to Applaud." New Republic, 30 July 1962, pp. 23-24, 26.

A review of Alfred Kazin's Contemporaries in which Heller counts the author's "chief weakness" in reading modern fiction "his unwillingness to enjoy it."

iii. Pynchon

73   "A Journey into the Mind of Watts." New York Times Magazine, 12 June 1966, pp. 34-35, 78, 80-82, 84.

An important essay on southern California: the only piece of non-fiction that Pynchon has ever published.

IV
Critical Books, Collections of Essays,
Special Numbers of Journals

i. Hawkes

77   Busch, Frederick. Hawkes: A Guide To His Fictions.
      Syracuse University Press, 1973.

      Prof. Busch's is the first full-length study of
      Hawkes' fiction. His main intention, which he realizes
      successfully, is to "show how Hawkes creates whole
      worlds of imagery," (p. ix) especially "the animal
      imagery that runs through his work from beginning to
      end." (p. xix). Prof. Busch calls Hawkes "the poet
      of our dread," and deals with the specific language
      of each novel, each carefully created fictive universe.
      Since the book is a guide, an attempt to elucidate
      approaches to complicated texts, and since its impor-
      tance lay in a close reading of some of Hawkes' most
      daring innovations, the chapters are at times uneven,
      but the quality of writing is high. Continuing a study
      initiated in graduate school (see his Columbia masters
      essay, "A John Hawkes Beastiary: Animal Imagery in the
      Novels of John Hawkes," 1967), Prof. Busch's readings
      of the early novels are superb: Charivari, The Canni-
      bal, The Beetle Leg, The Goose on the Grave. His brief-
      est and least successful chapters are those on The
      Lime Twig and Second Skin, though his longest, on The
      Blood Oranges, is very good. There is a brief chapter
      on The Innocent Party, and a bibliographical note.
      Missing is a reading of the short fiction. Death,
      Sleep & The Traveler and Travesty were published after
      this study.

78   Critique, 6/2(Fall, 1963). Hawkes and Barth issue.

      Contains (annotated in Sections V and VI):

78a   Trachtenberg, Alan. "Barth and Hawkes: Two Fabulists,"
         pp. 4-18.
78b   Guerard, Albert J. "The Prose Style of John Hawkes,"
         pp. 19-29.
78c   Reutlinger, D.P. "The Cannibal: 'The Reality of Vic-
         tim', " pp. 30-37.
78d   Matthews, Charles. "The Destructive Vision of John
         Hawkes," pp. 38-52.
78e   Bryer, Jackson. "Bibliography," pp. 89-94.

79   Critique, 17/3 (1976). Hawkes issue.

        Contains (annotated in Sections V and VI):

79a   Knapp, John V. "Hawkes' The Blood Oranges: A Sensual
        New Jerusalem," pp. 5-25.
79b   Greiner, Donald J. "Death, Sleep & The Traveler:
        Hawkes' Return to Terror," pp. 26-38.
79c   Kraus, Elizabeth. "Psychic Sores in Search of
        Compassion: Hawkes' Death, Sleep & The Traveler,"
        pp. 39-52.
79d   Plung, Daniel. "John Hawkes: A Selected Bibliography,"
        pp. 55-63.

80   Graham, John, ed. Studies in Second Skin. Columbus:
        Charles E. Merrill, 1971.

        Contains (annotated in Sections I, III and V):

80a   Graham, John. "Preface," pp. iii-vi.
80b   Five reviews of Second Skin (see #6), pp. 2-18.
80c   Hawkes, John. "Notes on The Wild Goose Chase,"
        pp. 20-30.
80d   Enck, John. "John Hawkes: An Interview," pp. 22-31.
80e   Graham, John. "John Hawkes: On His Novels," pp. 31-33.
80f   Kuehl, John. "Story into Novel," pp. 35-38.
80g   Hawkes, John. "The Nearest Cemetery," pp. 38-43.
80h   Oberbeck, S. K. "John Hawkes: The Smile Slashed by a
        Razor," pp. 45-52.
80i   Frost, Lucy. "Awakening Paradise," pp. 52-63.
80j   Robinson, William R. "John Hawkes' Artificial Insem-
        inator," pp. 63-69.
80k   Nichols, Stephen G., Jr. "Vision and Tradition in
        Second Skin," pp. 69-82.
80l   Santore, Anthony C. "Narrative Unreliability and the
        Structure of Second Skin," pp. 83-93.
80m   Guerard, Albert J. "Second Skin: The Light and Dark
        Affirmation," pp. 93-102.

81   Greiner, Donald J. Comic Terror: The Novels of John
        Hawkes. Memphis State University Press, 1973.

        Prof. Greiner's book is the most ambitious study of
        Hawkes' fiction yet published, appearing several
        months after Prof. Busch's Guide. Its aims are broad:
        "What I hope to accomplish . . . is a clarification of
        Hawkes' technique and comedy, and a study of each
        novel which will offer suggestions about many of the
        more troublesome passages and image patterns." (p.
        xviii). Thus, each chapter beyond the first, wherein
        a discussion of Hawkes' peculiar brand of "black
        comedy" takes place, is generated by several objec-
        tives, and, as a consequence, a tightness of focus is
        replaced by a many-layered explication of a novel.

        24

The results, at times, are immensely successful, as
his readings of the earlier, more dazzlingly experimental "comic" novels demonstrate, most notably his
chapter on The Beetle Leg. The analyses of the later
novels, from The Lime Twig on, are less galvanizing
in part because his thesis holds more tenuously when
applied to the "mature" fiction, and in part because
the prose and the argument become somewhat redundant.
There is a bibliography, but no discussion of the
short stories and plays. Death, Sleep & The Traveler
and Travesty were published after this study.

82   Harvard Advocate, 104/2 (October, 1970). Hawkes issue.

        Contains (annotated in Sections I, III, and V):

82a   Hawkes, John. "From a Forthcoming Novel," p. 5.
82b   Keyser, David, and Ned French. "Talks with John
          Hawkes," pp. 6, 34-35.
82c   Hawkes, John. "A Little Bit of the Old Slap and
          Tickle," pp. 7-8.
82d   Guerard, Albert J. "John Hawkes in English J," pp.
          10-11.
82e   Barth, John. "A Tribute to John Hawkes," p. 11.

83   Kuehl, John. John Hawkes and the Craft of Conflict.
          Rutgers University Press, 1975.

        Prof. Kuehl's is the latest and most specialized of
        the longer studies of Hawkes. Instead of engaging in
        a novel-by-novel reading, or a chronological pro-
        gression, Prof. Kuehl explores what he considers the
        most important of the "conceptual patterns" which
        unify Hawkes' oeuvre -- the "tension between Eros
        (love/life) and Thanatos (death) -- and, by assuming
        that "the form and content are inseparable" in Hawkes'
        fiction, this formalist study "treats the relationship
        between Hawkes' central theme and his craft, and
        simultaneously traces the evolution of both." (p. xi).
        Each chapter but the last, an extended reading of
        The Blood Oranges, is devoted to a different tech-
        nique, the focus moving from landscapes and settings,
        to myths and rituals, to structure and the use of
        time, to methods of characterization, and, finally,
        to the change in narrative focus from the predomi-
        nantly third-person earlier to the later first-person
        novels. Prof. Kuehl's thesis holds up well, although
        the internal movements within the chapters may be
        difficult to follow at times, and his is one of the
        finest descriptions of Hawkes' evolution as a novel-
        ist. The plays and the short stories are included in
        the discussion. Death, Sleep & The Traveler is dis-
        cussed in a brief postscript, and Travesty was pub-
        lished after this study.

84   Kiley, Frederick, and Walter McDonald, eds. A Catch-
      22 Casebook. New York: Crowell, 1973.

      Contains (annotated in Sections I, III, V, and VI):

84a   Kiley, Frederick, and Walter McDonald. "Preface,"
      pp. v-vi.
84b   Eleven reviews of Catch-22 (see #11), pp. 3-39.
84c   Wain, John. "A New Novel About Old Troubles,"pp. 43-49.
84d   Scammell, W. "Letter in Reply to Mr. Wain," pp. 49-50.
84e   Denniston, Constance. "Catch-22: A Romance Parody,"
      pp. 51-57.
84f   Milne, Victor J. "Heller's 'Bologniad': A Theological
      Perspective on Catch-22," pp. 58-73.
84g   Ritter, Jesse. "Fearful Comedy: Catch-22 as Avatar of
      the Social Surrealist Novel," pp. 73-86.
84h   Cheuse, Alan. "Laughing on the Outside," pp. 86-93.
84i   Solomon, Eric. "From Christ in Flanders to Catch-22:
      An Approach to War Fiction," pp. 94-101.
84j   MacDonald, James L. "I See Everything Twice!" The
      Structure of Joseph Heller's Catch-22," pp. 102-08.
84k   Mellard, James M. "Catch-22: Déjà vu and the Labyrinth
      of Memory," pp. 109-21.
84l   Solomon, Jan. "The Structure of Joseph Heller's
      Catch-22," pp. 122-132.
84m   Gaukroger, Doug. "Time Structure in Catch-22," pp.
      132-44.
84n   Stark, Howard J. "The Anatomy of Catch-22," pp. 145-58.
84o   Karl, Frederick R. "Joseph Heller's Catch-22: Only
      Fools Walk in Darkness," pp. 159-65.
84p   Doskow, Minna. "The Night Journey in Catch-22," pp.
      166-74.
84q   Castelli, Jim. "Catch-22 and the New Hero," pp. 174-81.
84r   Day, Douglas. "Catch-22: A Manifesto for Anarchists,"
      pp. 181-87.
84s   McK. Henry, G. B. "Significant Corn: Catch-22," pp.
      187-201.
84t   Protherough, Robert. "The Sanity of Catch-22," pp.
      201-12.
84u   Monk, Donald. "An Experiment in Therapy: A Study of
      Catch-22," pp. 212-20.
84v   Ramsey, Vance. "From Here to Absurdity: Heller's
      Catch-22," pp. 221-36.
84w   Podhoretz, Norman. "The Best Catch There Is," pp.
      237-41.
84x   Hunt, John W. "Comic Escape and Anti-Vision: Joseph
      Heller's Catch-22," pp. 242-47.
84y   Vos, Nelvin, "The Angel, the Beast, and the Machine,"

86   Scotto, Robert M., ed. A Critical Edition of Catch-22.
        New York: Delta, 1973.

        Contains (annotated in Sections I, III, V, and VI):

86a   Scotto, Robert M. "Introduction," pp. v-xi.
86b   The text of Catch-22, pp. 7-443.
86c   "Love, Dad," pp. 447-55.
86d   Krassner, Paul. "An Impolite Interview with Joseph
        Heller," pp. 456-78.
86e   Karl, Frederick R. "Joseph Heller's Catch-22: Only
        Fools Walk in Darkness," pp. 481-88.
86f   Kazin, Alfred. "The War Novel: From Mailer to Vonne-
        gut," pp. 488-91.
86g   Doskow, Minna. "The Night Journey in Catch-22," pp.
        491-500.
86h   Solomon, Jan. "The Structure of Joseph Heller's
        Catch-22," pp. 501-11.
86i   Mellard, James M. "Catch-22: Déjà vu and the Labyrinth
        Memory," pp. 512-25.
86j   Kennard, Jean. "Joseph Heller: At War with Absurdity,"
        pp. 526-41.
86k   Protherough, Robert. "The Sanity of Catch-22," pp.
        541-44.
86l   Blues, Thomas. "The Moral Structure of Catch-22,"
        pp. 544-59.
86m   "A Checklist of Critical Works on Catch-22," pp.
        560-62.

                          iii. Pynchon

87   Critique, 16/2 (1974). Pynchon issue.

        Contains (annotated in Section V):

87a   Patteson, Richard. "What Stencil Knew: Structure and
        Certitude in Pynchon's V.," pp. 30-44.
87b   Leland, John P. "Pynchon's Linguistic Demon: The
        Crying of Lot 49," pp. 45-53.
87c   Simmon, Scott. "Gravity's Rainbow Described," pp. 54-67.
87d   Simmon, Scott. "A Character Index: Gravity's Rainbow,"
        pp. 68-72.
87e   Ozier, Lance W. "Antipointsman/Antimexico: Some Mathe-
        matical Imagery in Gravity's Rainbow," pp. 73-90.

88   Levine, George, and David Leverenz, eds. Mindful
        Pleasures: Essays on Thomas Pynchon. Boston: Little,
        Brown, 1976.

        Contains (annotated in Sections V and VI):

88a   Levine, George and David Leverenz, "Introduction,"

pp. 3-11.
88b Poirier, Richard. "The Importance of Thomas Pynchon,"
     pp. 15-29.
88c Stimpson, Catherine R. "Pre-Apocalyptic Atavism:
     Thomas Pynchon's Early Fiction," pp. 31-47.
88d Tanner, Tony. "Caries and Cabals," pp. 49-67.
88e Lhamon, W. T. "Pentecost, Promiscuity, and Pynchon's
     V.: From the Scaffold to the Impulsive," pp. 69-86.
88f Mangel, Anne. "Maxwell's Demon, Entropy, Information:
     The Crying of Lot 49," pp. 87-100.
88g Vesterman, William. "Pynchon's Poetry," pp. 101-12.
88h Levine, George. "Risking the Moment: Anarchy and
     Possibility in Pynchon's Fiction," pp. 113-36.
88i Sanders, Scott. "Pynchon's Paranoid History," pp.
     139-59.
88j Mendelson, Edward. "Gravity's Encyclopedia," pp.
     161-95.
88k Kaufman, Marjorie. "Brunnhilde Among the Chemists,"
     pp. 197-227.
88l Leverenz, David. "On Trying to Read Gravity's Rain-
     bow," pp. 229-49.
88m Winston, Matthew. "The Quest for Pynchon," pp. 252-63.
88n Herzberg, Bruce. "Bibliography," pp. 265-69.

89   Slade, Joseph W. Thomas Pynchon. Writers for the 70's.
     New York: Warner, 1974.

     REVIEWED:
89a   Edward Mendelson. Times Literary Supplement, 13 June
       1975, p. 666.

An essential introduction to Pynchon's novels, the
only full-length study available, and the starting-
point for any that are to follow. Prof. Slade complains
that concentrating on "theme and plot" prevents him
from exploring other interesting areas: Pynchon's
"hyperdense metaphors, his felicities of style,"
and his humor. (p. 17). But nonetheless, what he does
he does well. His first chapter is a survey of the
few stories Pynchon has published and their relationship, especially by anticipation, to the novels. The
remainder of the book is a careful introduction to
the immense complexities of the novels. Chapters two
and three explore the dual structure of V., and especially effective is Prof. Slade's delineation of the
intricate relationship between the Profane and Stencil
chapters, the present and the past. Chapter four is
a most eloquent defense of The Crying of Lot 49, Pynchon's most overlooked book. Chapters five and six are
about the almost inexplicable Gravity's Rainbow, its
major themes, its uses of history, its innovative
exploration of science, technology and pop culture.
There is a brief, apologetic conclusion and a selective
bibliography.

90   <u>Twentieth Century Literature</u>, 21/2 (May, 1975). Pynchon issue, reprinted in <u>Mindful Pleasures</u>, eds.
Levine and Leverenz.

Contains (annotated in Sections V and VI):

90a   Levine, George and David Leverenz. "Introduction:
Mindful Pleasures," pp. iii-v.
90b   Poirier, Richard. "The Importance of Pynchon," pp.
151-62.
90c   Lhamon, W. T., Jr. "Pentecost, Promiscuity, and Pynchon's <u>V</u>.: From the Scaffold to the Impulsive,"
pp. 163-76.
90d   Sanders, Scott. "Pynchon's Paranoid History," pp.
177-92.
90e   Ozier, Lance W. "The Calculus of Transformation:
More Mathematical Imagery in <u>Gravity's Rainbow</u>,"
pp. 193-210.
90f   Vesterman, William. "Pynchon's Poetry," pp. 211-20.
90g   Herzberg, Bruce. "Selected Articles on Thomas Pynchon: An Annotated Bibliography," pp. 221-25.

V

Critical Essays and Chapters

i. Hawkes

a. General

91   "American Fiction: The Postwar Years, 1945-1965." Book
     Week, 26 September 1965, pp. 1-3, 5-7, 18, 20, 22,
     24-25.

     A potpourri of observations and opinions resulting
     from a poll. Hawkes is mentioned briefly as an
     important novelist, and he responded to the question-
     naire in a brief paragraph by saying that postwar
     American fiction "has developed mainly in terms of
     verbal and visionary liberation."

92   Barth, John. "Having It Both Ways: A Conversation
     Between John Barth and Joe David Bellamy." New
     American Review, 15 (1972), 134-50.

     REPRINTED:
92a The New Fiction: Interviews With Innovative Ameri-
     can Writers, ed. Joe David Bellamy. University of
     Illinois Press, 1974, pp. 1-18.

     A brief mention of Hawkes as, to Barth, "among the
     living grand masters."

93   Barth, John. "A Tribute to John Hawkes." Harvard Advo-
     cate, 104/2 (October, 1970), 11.

     A brief recognition of the "integrity" of Hawkes'
     "voice and painful grace of his conceits," which
     "are standards by which most recent American fiction
     is revealed." He concludes: "There's not one I more
     admire."

94   Blau, Herbert. "Preface" to The Innocent Party. New
     York: New Directions, 1967, pp. 9-12.

     A tribute to Hawkes both as a dramatist and an
     interested participant in the San Francisco pro-
     ductions of his plays.

95   Buckeye, Robert. "The Anatomy of the Psychic Novel."
     Critique, 9/2 (1967), 33-45.

In a discussion of fiction that "sees reality to be multiple and uncertain," Hawkes is mentioned briefly.

96   Dunn, Douglas. "Profile 11: John Hawkes." New Review, 1 (March, 1975), 23-28.

A good general introduction of Hawkes, the man and the work, for the British reading public.

97   Fiedler, Leslie. "A Lonely American Eccentric: The Pleasures of John Hawkes." New Leader, 12 December 1960, pp. 12-14.

REPRINTED:
97a   "Introduction" to The Lime Twig. New York: New Directions, 1961, pp. vii-xiv. Enlarged.
97b   The Collected Essays of Leslie Fiedler. New York: Stein and Day, 1971, II, 319-24.

A discussion of Hawkes as a "Gothic novelist" with special emphasis on The Lime Twig. He notes that, in 1960, Hawkes is the "lonely eccentric" of American letters, "the least read novelist of substantial merit in the United States."

98   Friedman, Melvin J. "John Hawkes and Flannery O'Connor: The French Background." Boston University Journal, 21/3 (1973), 34-44.

A study both of the relationship between Hawkes and O'Connor, one of the writers he has always credited with admiration, as well as the influence of French avant-garde writers upon both of them.

99   Frohock, W. M. "How Hawkes' Humor Works." Southwest Review, 59 (Summer, 1974), 330-32.

A review both of Greiner's book on Hawkes, Comic Terror, and Death, Sleep & The Traveler: a favorable response to the critical work, a less favorable response to the novel, which, unlike the early works of Hawkes -- when he was "at his best" because he was "closest to the spirit of the grotesque painter" -- "disconcerted"him "far too little."

100   Frohock, W. M. "John Hawkes' Vision of Violence." Southwest Review, 50/1 (Winter, 1965), 69-79.

A discussion of the "fabric of deep-textured nightmare" Hawkes weaves through his novels up to Second Skin. He concludes that Hawkes, who is doing "something seriously new in fiction," is read "only for the pleasure of following a hypersensitive

imagination as it faces the fact of existence,
which is a pleasure only from the novel."

101 Greiner, Donald. "Strange Laughter: The Comedy of
     John Hawkes." Southwest Review, 56/4 (Autumn,
     1971), 318-28.

     A discussion of the difference between the "laugh-
     ter" in modern fiction and the traditional sources
     of comedy. Since Hawkes dismisses the "utilitarian"
     concept of humor," for stability and standardiza-
     tion have disappeared, his comedy is grotesque,
     nightmarish, unemotional. Second Skin best illus-
     trates his "immersion" in chaos.

102 Guerard, Albert J. "The Illuminating Distortion."
     Novel, 5/2 (Winter, 1972), 101-21.

     In contrast to the "precise explanation" of classic
     novels, the moment of revelation, of "strangeness"
     in much contemporary fiction occurs in an "illumin-
     ating distortion." After textual analyses of several
     novels, both old and new, Prof. Guerard briefly
     touches on the "tragic situations" in Second Skin
     and The Blood Oranges (pp. 115-16).

103 Guerard, Albert J. "Introduction to the Cambridge
     Anti-Realists." Audience, 7 (Spring, 1960), 57-59.

     An introduction to several sections from novels,
     including The Lime Twig, whose authors share certain
     similarities, including "visionary and destructive
     impulses" and "frank and grotesque distortion."
     Hawkes, argues Prof. Guerard, although he is
     becoming "more conscious and controlled," still
     maintains his "primitive power to evoke another
     world beyond the world we think we see."

104 Guerard, Albert J. "John Hawkes in English J." Harvard
     Advocate, 104/2 (October, 1970), 10-11.

     An account of Hawkes as a student in creative
     writing, his early career in general, and the gene-
     sis of Charivari and The Cannibal in particular.

105 Guerard, Albert J. "Notes on the Rhetoric of Anti-
     Realist Fiction." Tri-Quarterly, 30 (Spring, 1974),
     3-50.

     A long essay in which Prof. Guerard analyzes the
     styles used by anti-realists, writers "determined
     to re-imagine the world or create a new one." He
     notes that Hawkes' (pp. 31-36) strengths lie "in

the intense uncontrived and menacing observed outer
world and an inner world of childhood fears still
wonderfully alive," and in that the images and
mythologies of "Freudian process" are "personae"
in his fictional world.

106   Guerard, Albert J. "The Prose Style of John Hawkes."
       Critique, 6/2 (Fall, 1963), 19-29.

       A discussion of "one of the most personal of con-
       temporary prose styles" which has moved from "murky,
       groping, brilliant, eccentric expression to deliber-
       ate rhetorical manipulation of the reader's anxieties
       and sympathies." Prof. Guerard concentrates on
       Hawkes's "relative abandonment of 'literary' dis-
       play," his "appeal of irony and control," his com-
       plex "voice," and his rich "verbal inventions."

107   Hassan, Ihab H. "The Character of Post-War Fiction in
       America." English Journal, 51 (January, 1962), 1-8.

       REPRINTED:
107a   On Contemporary Literature, ed. Richard Kostelanetz.
       New York: Avon, 1969, pp. 36-47.
107b   Recent American Fiction, ed. Joseph Waldmeir. Boston:
       Houghton-Mifflin, 1963, pp. 27-35.

       Hawkes is singled out frequently as a significant
       voice in this survey.

108   Hassan, Ihab. Contemporary American Literature, 1945-
       1972: An Introduction. New York: Ungar, 1973, pp.
       52-54.

       A brief survey and general overview of a career of
       "narrow art" fully realized through a "bizarre
       poetic sensibility," a "satirical impulse," and an
       original language.

109   Koch, Stephen. "Circling Hawkes." Saturday Review/World,
       1 June 1975, pp. 20-22.

       An appreciation of "the visionary places and spaces
       of the fragmented twentieth-century terrain" which
       Hawkes renders "magical, dangerous, unearthly, by
       imagined transformations." Although he is not over-
       whelmed by The Blood Oranges or Death, Sleep & The
       Traveler, he considers The Beetle Leg a masterpiece
       wherein Hawkes "is fully in command of his fictional
       voice," -- the one novel of his "that must be in-
       cluded in the list of very great writing done by
       Americans in this century."

110   Levine, Paul. "The Intemperate Zone: The Climate of

34

Contemporary American Fiction." <u>Massachusetts Review</u>, 8/2 (Spring, 1967), 505-23.

The "distress" we feel behind the "affluence" of contemporary life is reflected in our fiction, the novels of Hawkes being one of many illustrations.

111   Littlejohn, David. "The Anti-Realists." <u>Daedalus</u>, 92/2 (Spring, 1963), 250-64.

In a discussion of the "novel of fantasy, illogicality and absurdity," of "fiction of the dreaming, subconscious self," Hawkes is singled out as the "purest" example of the anti-realistic novelist among those discussed (pp. 256-58).

112   Loukides, Paul. "The Radical Vision." <u>Michigan Academician</u>, 5 (1973), 497-503.

Hawkes is mentioned briefly in this survey of radical writers.

113   Malin, Irving. <u>Psychoanalysis and American Fiction</u>. New York: Dutton, 1965, pp. 271-75.

In a chapter entitled "The Gothic Family" Hawkes' treatment of unorthodox familial relations through <u>Second Skin</u> is discussed.

114   Malin, Irving. <u>New American Gothic</u>. Carbondale: Southern Illinois University Press, 1962, pp. 9-10, 38-44, 71-75, 99-103, 124-26, 159-60.

A discussion of Hawkes' fiction through <u>The Lime Twig</u>, centering on his use of animalistic imagery, his portrayal of the child in conflict with the adult world, his "fiction of entrapment in private underworlds," and his "out-of-focus" fiction as emblematic of the new American Gothic.

115   Matthews, Charles. "The Destructive Vision of John Hawkes." <u>Critique</u>, 6/2 (Fall, 1963), 38-52.

"Hawkes has mastered the art of recreating dream experience and its terrible reality," Prof. Matthews explains. Hawkes' technique -- "to destroy the conventional linkages and unifying forces of narrative" -- is then applied to the novels through <u>The Lime Twig</u>, and the conclusion drawn that the vision of degredation that results "must be taken seriously" since the "tenuousness and ephemerality" of experience has been brilliantly delineated.

116   Nin, Anais. <u>The Novel of the Future</u>. New York: Macmillan, 1968, pp. 176-78.

The author disagrees with Prof. Guerard's preference
for Hawkes over Djuna Barnes: "The world of the critic
is...masculine...a one-party world."

117   Oberbeck, S. K. "John Hawkes: The Smile Slashed by a
       Razor," in Contemporary American Novelists, ed.
       Harry T. Moore. Carbondale: Southern Illinois
       University Press, 1964, pp. 193-204.

       REPRINTED:
117a   Studies in Second Skin, ed. John Graham, pp. 45-52.

       A discussion of the humor in Hawkes which works with
       "the heart of darkness" at the core of his vision to
       produce the "matchless disrespect for our habitual
       reading expectations" and the "purely creative
       settings" of his fiction. Hawkes' mixture of "pity
       and exhilaration" results in "a viewpoint held by
       few American authors.

118   O'Brien, John. "The Hawkes Industry." Novel, 10/1
       (Fall, 1976), 85-87.

       A review of three critical works on Hawkes, those
       by Greiner (highly praised), Busch and Kuehl (less
       kindly received).

119   Ratner, Marc. "The Constructed Vision: The Fiction of
       John Hawkes." Studi Americani, 11 (1965), 345-57.

       An overview of Hawkes' fiction through The Lime
       Twig, but centering on The Cannibal as an example
       of "the ironic vision of twentieth century man"
       viewed "through the imagination of the poet and the
       objectivity of the novelist."

120   Romano, John. "Our Best-Known Neglected Novelist."
       Commentary, 58/5 (May, 1974), 58-60.

       In part a review of Death, Sleep & The Traveler,
       in part an assessment of Hawkes' career. Prof.
       Romano believes that Second Skin is more powerful
       than Death because it is more "realistic." With
       The Blood Oranges Hawkes has "tended towards the
       obliquity and self-conscious artificiality that
       are now so fashionable."

121   Rosenfeld, Claire. "John Hawkes: Nightmares of the
       Real." Minnesota Review, 2/2 (Winter, 1962), 249-54.

       A long review of The Lime Twig as well as a recapitu-
       lation of Hawkes' career. Prof. Rosenfeld concludes:
       "The movement from The Cannibal to The Lime Twig,
       while it reveals an elimination of some gratuitous
       horror and a few private images, also manifests a

more subtle control of symbolism."

122   Rovit, Earl. "The Fiction of John Hawkes: An Intro-
        ductory View." Modern Fiction Studies, 11/2 (Summer,
        1964), 150-62.

        A good general overview of the accomplishment of
        John Hawkes through The Lime Twig, especially his
        fictional techniques.

123   Schott, Webster. "John Hawkes, American Original."
        New York Times Book Review, 29 May 1966, pp. 4, 24-25.

        An overview of the novels of Hawkes through Second
        Skin, which, "like private static truths," "form a
        whole continually in motion." A laudatory appraisal
        which concludes: "Through creation more astonishing
        than any representation 'of reality,' he has caught
        the rhythm of our secret processes."

124   Skerrett, Joseph Taylor, Jr. "Dostoievsky, Nathanael
        West, and Some Contemporary American Fiction."
        University of Dayton Review, 4/1 (1967), 23-36.

        A brief mention of Hawkes.

125   Spencer, Sharon. Space, Time and Structure in the
        Modern Novel. Chicago: Swallow, 1971, pp. 29-32,
        82-84, 88-90, passim.

        A brief but poignant notation on "some of the most
        terrifying closed worlds in modern fiction," the
        novels The Cannibal, Second Skin and The Lime Twig.

126   Stubbs, John C. "John Hawkes and the Dream-Work of
        The Lime Twig and Second Skin." Language and Psychol-
        ogy, 21 (1971), 149-60.

        A long study of Hawkes' special use of dreams, dream-
        ing, and, especially, dream language in the two novels.

127   Tanner, Tony. "Necessary Landscapes and Luminous
        Deteriorations." TriQuarterly, 20 (1971), 145-79.

        REPRINTED:
127a   City of Words. New York: Harper and Row, 1971, pp.
        202-29.

        An extensive discussion of Hawkes' attempt "to
        build and fix a landscape" in each of his novels
        through Second Skin. The later novels are moving
        towards what appears to be "a more conventional
        narrative line" in keeping with Hawkes' intention
        to parody conventional fiction. A lucid delineation.

128   Trachtenberg, Alan. "Barth and Hawkes: Two Fabulists."
       Critique, 6/2 (Fall, 1963), 4-18.

       A discussion of two apparently "widely dissimilar"
       writers who share, among other things, a craft that
       is "respectively hard, original, and difficult."
       Each is a "fabulist" who invents "form according to
       the logic of his own genius," but Hawkes especially
       invests meaning in "obscurity of life," writing
       fictions that are "pure ambience, verging on
       poetry."

129   Widmer, Kingsley. The Literary Rebel. Carbondale:
       Southern Illinois University Press, 1965, pp. 234,
       38.

       A brief discussion of Hawkes as a "gothic experi-
       mental."

                         b. The Cannibal

130   Fiedler, Leslie. Love and Death in the American
       Novel. New York: Criterion, 1960, pp. 467-68.

       A brief discussion of the "surrealism" of The
       Cannibal and its indirect relationship to Djuna
       Barnes' Nightwood.

131   Guerard, Albert J. "Introduction" to The Cannibal.
       Norfolk: New Directions, 1949, pp. ix-xvi.
       Addendum to New Directions Paperbook, 1962, pp.
       xvii-xx.

       A discussion of Hawkes' methods and difficulties
       for an audience which, in 1948, was first intro-
       duced to an "independent surrealism." This original
       work of art, Prof. Guerard contends, more than
       amply repays the "peripheral difficulties" first
       encountered.

132   Hassan, Ihab. "The Existential Novel." Massachusetts
       Review, 3/4 (Summer, 1962), 795-97.

       The existential novel -- "a world devoid of any pre-
       suppositions," whose hero creates "dignity out of
       humiliation," and whose "form is ironic" -- is
       illustrated by Hawkes' The Cannibal, among other
       works.

133   Reutlinger, D. P. "The Cannibal: 'The Reality of
       Victim'. " Critique, 6/2 (Fall, 1963), 30-37.

       The Cannibal is the "most comprehensive" vision
       of "cyclical depersonalized disaster" Hawkes has

                              38

realized. In the "anonymous nation" which survived
the war, "the entire community has lost all conscious sense of its past self." Prof. Reutlinger
concludes: "just as the Cannibal becomes eponymous
for the perverted romantic community of victims,
so also does cannibalism become the stark control-
ling image of Hawkes' dark art. Ethics and aesthetics are one."

134   Vickery, Olga W. "The Inferno of the Moderns," in
       The Shaken Realist, eds. Melvin J. Friedman and
       John B. Vickery. Baton Rouge: Louisiana State
       University Press, 1970, pp. 147-64.

       A brief discussion of The Cannibal (pp. 153-55) as
       a novel about a Dantesque "city of the living dead."
       Hawkes' originality is constituted by his "fusion
       of realistic detail, psychological acumen, and
       controlled fantasy."

                    c. Charivari

135   Green, James L. "Nightmare and Fairy Tale in Hawkes'
       'Charivari'." Critique, 13/1 (1971), 83-95.

       A discussion of Charivari as a work "cast in the
       form of a fairy tale," "a nightmare with a happy
       ending," but presented ironically so that the
       result is "affirming the reality of nightmare" at
       the same time. Although a more "tenuous"book than
       The Cannibal, Charivari is still an impressive
       tale about how "repressed human impulses reassert
       themselves in tormenting nightmare and neurosis."

                    d. The Beetle Leg

136   Frost, Lucy. "The Drowning of the Merican Adam:
       Hawkes' The Beetle Leg." Critique, 14/3 (1972),
       63-74.

       Within the stasis of a Hawkes novel, caused by his
       "remote literary style," his "refusal to create
       psychological complexity," and his "refusal to
       structure his narrative according to conventional
       plots," is a dramatic tension "between language
       and subject matter" clearly present in The Beetle
       Leg, whose mythic substructure is "the biblical
       myth of Adam's fall together with the peculiarly
       American cultural myth of the new Eden."

                    e. The Lime Twig

137   Boutrous, Lawrence K. "Parody in Hawkes' The Lime
       Twig." Critique, 15/2 (1973), 49-56.

An analysis of the novel as a parody of both "the thriller" and "the detective story." Hawkes "uses parody because it is the best vehicle with which to extend the form of the novel, creating at once an ambivalent world of destruction and hope."

138 Edenbaum, Robert I. "John Hawkes: The Lime Twig and Other Tenuous Horrors." Massachusetts Review, 7/3 (Summer, 1966), 462-75.

A comparison of The Lime Twig and West's The Day of the Locust. The textual analysis concentrates on Hawkes' manipulation of violence, "man's best as well as his worst," which account both for "creativity" as well as "destructiveness." For West, the horrors had been "unambiguously futile," however; for Hawkes, they are "unambiguously triumphant."

139 Frohock, W. M. "The Failing Center: Recent Fiction and the Picaresque Tradition." Novel, 3/1 (Fall, 1969), 62-69.

A discussion of the problematical nature of the term "picaresque," with some reference to The Lime Twig: Hawkes' "coldness," "detachment," and affinity for the "potential failure within ourselves and in the world around us" are considered.

140 Olderman, Raymond M. Beyond the Waste Land: A Study of American Novels in the Nineteen-Sixties. New Haven: Yale University Press, 1972, pp. 150-75, and passim.

Hawkes "explores the individual's dream, and the violent terror -- the lust for death -- that haunts the heart of that dream," unlike more "public" writers like Heller and Pynchon. In The Lime Twig Michael Banks "is literally run over by a power evoked from his own unconscious desires in conspiracy with a malevolent external force." Like The Waste Land, this novel is "constructed from a mixture of memory and desire."

141 Shepard, Allen. "Illumination Through (Anti) Climax: John Hawkes' The Lime Twig." Notes on Contemporary Literature, 2/2 (1972), 11-13.

A brief study of the ending of The Lime Twig.

142 Scholes, Robert. The Fabulators. New York: Oxford University Press, 1967, pp. 59-94.

An extensive and searching discussion of Hawkes'

"black humor," and an extensive exegesis on The
Lime Twig. This novel of the "interconnections
between cruelty and tenderness" is "a richer,
more complex mode of narrative" than his earlier
fiction, and "as neatly and tightly put together
as the electrical circuitry of the human nervous
system."

143 Schott, Webster. "Vision of Nightmare." Nation, 2
     September 1961, pp. 122-23.

     A favorable review of The Lime Twig and Hawkes'
     career, the "complex allegories and private
     renderings of post-Freudian psychological insight"
     of "an American original." The Lime Twig has both
     "the terror of the nightmare" and "the unassail-
     ability of truth."

144 Warner, John M. "The 'Internalized Quest Romance'
     in Hawkes' The Lime Twig." Modern Fiction Studies,
     19/1 (Spring, 1973), 89-95.

     The world of The Lime Twig is not "our ordinary
     world" but one established "in its underlying
     myth," a myth "adumbrated in the novel's literary
     allusions." This "internalized quest romance,"
     therefore, suggests how difficult it is for modern
     man "to achieve that kind of consciousness which
     will free him to participate meaningfully in a
     transformed world of nature."

                    f. Second Skin

145 Frost, Lucy. "Awakening Paradise," in Studies in
     Second Skin, ed. John Graham, pp. 52-63.

     A discussion of the recurring action of "the voyage"
     which provides "structural unity" for Second Skin.
     Skipper's literal voyages are counterpointed by the
     pattern of allusions to The Tempest which creates
     the "pastoral romance" on the wandering isle, thus
     allaying the threat of Thanatos with Eros.

146 Galloway, David D. "Clown and Saint: The Hero in
     Current American Fiction." Critique, 7 (Spring/
     Summer, 1965), 46-65.

     Briefly touches upon Skipper in Second Skin (pp.
     53-54) as an example of the character of the comed-
     ian-redeemer so prevalent in contemporary fiction.

147 Greiner, Donald J. "The Thematic Use of Color in John
     Hawkes' Second Skin." Contemporary Literature, 11/3
     (Summer, 1970), 389-400.

                          41

An argument for structure: "The primary events in
the lives of the characters are purposely constructed to be dissociated from the limitations of chronological time and rational motive, but Hawkes' use
of color imposes unity on these seemingly unconnected
incidents." Variations on two pairs of colors, green
and yellow, black and white, dominate the novel.

148   Guerard, Albert J. "Second Skin: The Light and Dark
       Affirmation," in Studies in Second Skin, ed. John
       Graham, pp. 93-102.

       A discussion of the "most ambitious" and "warmest"
       of Hawkes' novels through an analysis of the inter-
       twining of bright and dark visions. Second Skin is
       the "culmination" of Hawkes' development, with its
       "controlled and conscious use of myth and fairy
       story," to its "exploitation, at once terrifying
       and wonderfully comic, of menacing sexual materials."

149   Hanzo, T. A. "The Two Faces of Matt Donelson." Se-
       wanee Review, 73 (Winter, 1965), 106-19.

       In a review of contemporary fiction, Second Skin
       is discussed (pp. 111-14) and its "stylistic
       excesses" recommended.

150   Imhoff, Ron. "On Second Skin." Mosaic, 8/1 (Fall, 1974),
       51-61. "Response" by John Hawkes, pp. 61-63.

       A study of the structure of the novel by referring
       to poetic language's "foregrounding" and its
       creation of inner tension: Skipper's "triumph"
       is his "distortion of the narrative norm."
       Hawkes explains that he was influenced by the
       "culpable narrators" in Gide's The Immoralist and
       Ford's The Good Soldier, and speaks briefly of
       Death, Sleep & The Traveler and its problematic
       narrator.

151   Kuehl, John, ed. Write and Rewrite: A Study of the
       Creative Process. New York: Meredith, 1967, pp.
       265, 284-87.

       REPRINTED:
151a   Studies in Second Skin, ed. John Grahan, pp. 33-38.

       Taking as his point of departure a letter from
       Hawkes, Prof. Kuehl analyzes the growth of Second
       Skin out of the short story "The Nearest Cemetery."

152   Lavers, Norman. "The Structure of Second Skin."
       Novel, 5/3 (Spring, 1972), 208-14.

A discussion of Second Skin as a parody of "The
Great American Novel itself," and an irreverent
commentary on attempts to define it in books like
Chase's The American Novel and its Tradition and
Fiedler's Love and Death in the American Novel,
which enumerate "its persistent and diagnostic
characteristics and concerns."

153 LeClair, Thomas. "Death and Black Humor." Critique,
     17/1 (1975), 5-40.

     "In Second Skin death is both the cause and the
     effect of man's fictionalizing reality," for Hawkes'
     method of narration, and his "brutal" comedy, pro-
     duce "the incongruity of Skipper's conception of
     himself and the reality he allows to be revealed."
     (pp. 19-21)

154 LeClair, Thomas. "John Hawkes' 'Death of an Airman'
     and Second Skin." Notes on Contemporary Litera-
     ture, 4/1 (January, 1974), 2-3.

     A brief discussion of the relationship between
     the early story and the novel, published fifteen
     years later.

155 LeClair, Thomas. "The Unreliability of Innocence:
     John Hawkes' Second Skin." Journal of Narrative
     Technique, 3/1 (January, 1973), 32-39.

     A discussion of Skipper as the unreliable narrator
     who "weaves a rhetorical fabric so engaging in
     its exquisite futility and sensibility that it
     becomes a net to trap the unwary reader." The
     paradoxical conclusion results from the reader's
     vacillation between thinking Hawkes is engaging
     in parody or presenting an affirmative vision.

156 Levine, Paul. "Individualism and the Individual
     Talent." Hudson Review, 17 (Autumn, 1964), 470-77.

     Within a general review of a large number of con-
     temporary novels, Second Skin is called a "snake's-
     eye view of a spiritual underworld" that is "often
     verbally exciting and visually rewarding."

157 Madden, David. "Enemies of Love." Kenyon Review, 26/3
     (Summer, 1964), 576-81.

     A review of Second Skin and several other novels.
     The energy of the novel, which comes from "the
     interplay of charged images of carnage and fructi-
     fication, love and sexual violence," is its appeal.
     Although "one senses a rhetorical self-indulgence"

43

and "the self-congratulation of a highly literary
sensibility," the book is still "a rare experience."

158   Nichols, Stephen C., Jr. "Vision and Tradition in
       Second Skin," in Studies in Second Skin, ed. John
       Graham, pp. 69-82.

       A study of the influence of Edwin Honig's Gazabos
       on Second Skin as well as the other "literary
       resonances" (Homer, Shakespeare, Dante) in the
       novel. Prof. Nichols also discusses the effect of
       the first person narrator on the theme of the
       "discovery of the self by the self."

159   Pearce, Richard. Stages of the Clown. Carbondale:
       Southern Illinois University Press, 1970, pp. 102-
       116.

       A discussion of Second Skin centering on the nature
       of Skipper as a "clown," but one "with complete
       self-awareness." Hawkes' "vulnerable" narrator
       eventually "dissolves reality."

160   Ricks, Christopher. "Chamber of Horrors." New States-
       man, 11 March 1966, pp. 339-40.

       A review of the British edition of Second Skin:
       unlike most "modern Gothic novelists," Hawkes ("a
       caricaturist rather than a parodist") owes his
       success to "his ability to make classical mythology
       take the place of that shared superstition . . .
       responsible for the hectic rhetoric of terror."

61   Robinson, William R. "John Hawkes' Artificial Insem-
       inator," in Studies in Second Skin, ed. John
       Graham, pp. 63-69.

       A study of Second Skin as a pastoral novel which
       illustrates the "proper relation between art and
       life": "a vital and vigorous bond between energy
       and form is the proper good of the imagination."

162   Santore, Anthony C. "Narrative Unreliability and the
       Structure of Second Skin," in Studies in Second
       Skin, ed. John Graham, pp. 83-93.

       A discussion of Skipper as an unreliable narrator
       who uses self-deception as a protective layer, or
       second skin, to shield himself from life's un-
       pleasantness. The ending, therefore, in peace
       emphasizes his successes while playing down his
       failures.

163   Trachtenberg, Stanley. "Counterhumor: Comedy in
       Contemporary American Fiction." Georgia Review,
       27/1 (Spring, 1973), 33-48.

       Second Skin is discussed briefly (pp.
       40-42): "the comic affirmation of the artificial is echoed in the
       narrative style as well as developed in thematic
       content."

164   Yarborough, Richard. "Hawkes' Second Skin." Mosaic,
       8/1 (Fall, 1974), 65-73.
       "Response" by John Hawkes, pp. 73-75.

       A discussion of Skipper as the "creator artist,
       ordering and manipulating his materials," through
       analogies to Berryman's Dream Songs especially.
       Hawkes discusses the religious elements of his
       novel and his desire not to "mythologize" death.

                   g. The Blood Oranges

165   Cuddy, Lois A. "Functional Pastoralism in The Blood
       Oranges." Studies in American Fiction, 3/1 (Spring,
       1975), 15-25.

       A study of the "essential function of pastoralism
       which is central to the structural and philosophical
       integrity" of The Blood Oranges. Prof. Cuddy con-
       cludes: "this new Illyrian myth" has at its center
       the "potentially pastoral man": Cyril.

166   Knapp, John V. "Hawkes' The Blood Oranges: A Sensual
       New Jerusalem." Critique, 17/3 (1973), 5-25.

       A discussion of Hawkes' "new" morality replacing
       "the outworn asexuality of a moribund Christianity."
       Several key scenes (discussed at length) transform
       Cyril into "the lordly fertility god" who recognizes
       that "sex and death must coexist."

167   Moran, Charles. "John Hawkes: Paradise Gaining."
       Massachusetts Review, 12/4 (Autumn, 1971), 840-45.

       A highly favorable review of The Blood Oranges as
       "another step in the writer's long journey out of
       the waste land," and as Hawkes' "comic lyric poem
       in prose."

                h. Death, Sleep & The Traveler

168   Greiner, Donald J. "Death, Sleep & The Traveler: John
       Hawkes' Return to Terror." Critique, 17/3 (1976),
       26-38.

Although recent Hawkes novels had been directed
away from "the comic terror" of the earlier ones,
this is a "truly terrifying book." Hawkes' use
of the sea and the ocean liner -- images that have
haunted him in the past -- make Allert's prospects
"especially grim."

169   Kraus, Elizabeth. "Psychic Sores in Search of Compas-
      sion: Hawkes' Death, Sleep & The Traveler."
      Critique, 17/3 (1976), 39-52.

The underlying theme of Hawkes' seventh novel is
"the conflict between the rational, judgmental
ego and the irrational, imaginative id of our
culture-repressed unconscious. "Allert is a middle
aged homosexual who committed murder in his youth
and who becomes "a compelling image of the twentieth-century man who, bruised by reality, can find
solace only in his imagination."

                    ii. Heller

170   Aichinger, Peter. The American Soldier in Fiction,
      1880-1963. Ames, Iowa: Iowa State University Press,
      1975, passim.

A discussion of Heller's treatment of "absurd" war,
the "non-hero," black humor and "the war novel as
pop art."

171   Aldridge, John. "Contemporary Fiction and Mass Culture."
      New Orleans Review, 1 (1968), 4-9.

A brief note on Catch-22.

172   Alter, Robert. "The Apocalyptic Temper." Commentary,
      41/5 (June, 1966), 61-66.

A reaction to R. W. B. Lewis' Trials of the Word:
Catch-22 is written in the "distinctively American
version" of apocalyptic literature: "the imagined
end of all things is in this elaborately ironic
presentation ludicrous as well as disturbing."

173   "American Fiction: The Postwar Years, 1945-1965."
      Book Week, 26 September 1965, pp. 1-3, 5-7, 18, 20,
      22, 24-25.

A potpourri of observations and opinions resulting
from a poll. Catch-22 is cited as one of the twenty
best postwar American novels (number 11); Heller
responded to the questionnaire by saying that of all

modern writers Faulkner and Steinbeck have the best chance of enduring.

174　"American Humor: Hardly a Laughing Matter." Time, 4 March 1966, pp. 46-47.

A brief mention of Catch-22 in a general essay.

175　Barksdale, Richard K. "Alienation and the Anti-Hero in Recent American Fiction." CLA Journal, 10 September, 1966), 1-10.

Brief mention of Catch-22.

176　Barnes, Hazel. "Literature and the Politics of the Future." Denver Quarterly, 5/1 (Spring, 1970), 41-64.

A brief reference to Catch-22 (pp. 48-49) is included in a discussion of fiction which "in its response to the contemporary situation seeks to point the way toward a different kind of future."

177　Barth, John. "Having It Both Ways: A Conversation Between John Barth and Joe David Bellamy." New American Review, 15 (1972), 134-50.

REPRINTED:
177a　The New Fiction: Interviews With Innovative American Writers, ed. Joe David Bellamy. University of Illinois Press, 1974, pp. 1-18.

A brief mention of Heller as among "the landmark writers more often than not . . . not formally or technically innovative."

178　Bergonzi, Bernard. The Situation of the Novel. University of Pittsburgh Press, 1970, pp. 82-86 and passim.

A discussion of Catch-22 and the absurdist or "comic-apocalyptic" school of novelists characterized by the interplay of two "opposed impulses," the first "realistic," the second "transcending."

179　Bier, Jesse. The Rise and Fall of American Humor. New York: Holt, Rinehart and Winston, 1968, pp. 346-47 and passim.

The "zaniness" of Catch-22 "exceeds that of the Marx Brothers," and is marred by "direct self-contradictions and shameless reversalisms."

180　"The Black Humorists." Time, 12 February 1965, pp. 94-96.

Catch-22 is discussed briefly in a general essay
on several contemporary novelists.

181   Blues, Thomas. "The Moral Structure of Catch-22."
       Studies in the Novel, 3 (Spring, 1971), 64-97.

       REPRINTED:
181a   A Critical Edition of Catch-22, ed. Robert M. Scotto,
       pp. 544-59.
181b   Critical Essays on Catch-22, ed. James Nagel, pp.
       102-16.

       Although Yossarian maintains the principle of life
       in a dehumanized world, argues Prof. Blues, at the
       very moment this affirmation should take place, his
       desertion, the novel's metaphors are abandoned for
       a "mechanically complete" action which betrays its
       careful craft.

182   Brewer, Joseph E. "The Anti-Hero in Contemporary
       Literature." Iowa English Yearbook, 12 (1967), 55-
       60.

       A brief mention of Catch-22.

183   Bryant, Jerry H. The Open Decision: The Contemporary
       American Novel and Its Intellectual Background.
       New York: The Free Press, 1970, pp. 156-64.

       An explication of Heller's theme of "survival through
       defiance." Better than any other war novel Catch-22
       illustrates how the individual "must be free to grow
       toward his own novel end."

184   Buckeye, Robert. "The Anatomy of the Psychic Novel."
       Critique, 9/2 (1967), 33-45.

       The psychic novel "sees reality to be multiple and
       uncertain; presents a protagonist who is conscious
       of the masks he wears in the world; and dramatizes
       the unceasing struggle between them." Catch-22 is
       discussed briefly (pp. 37-38).

185   Burgess, Anthony. "The Postwar American Novel: A
       View From the Periphery." American Scholar, 35/1
       (Winter, 1965/66), 150-56.

       A brief mention of Catch-22, passim, as one of the
       most representative novels of an exciting era in
       fiction.

186   Burhans, Clinton S., Jr. "Spindrift and the Sea:
       Structural Patterns and Unifying Elements in Catch-
       22." Twentieth Century Literature, 19/4 (October,

1973), 239-50.

A discussion of the "central conflict" -- Yossarian's
effort to avoid duty and, thus, get killed -- the
two "subplots"-- the struggle between Peckem and
Dreedle, Milo's syndicate -- and the "host of motifs"
as well as the "foreshadowing" flashback in Catch-22.

187   Byrd, Scott. "A Separate War: Camp and Black Humor in
      Recent American Fiction." Language Quarterly, 7/1
      and 2 (Fall/Winter, 1968), 7-10.

      A brief mention of Catch-22.

188   Castelli, Jim. "Catch-22 and the New Hero." Catholic
      World, 211 (July, 1970), 199-202.

      REPRINTED:
188a   A Catch-22 Casebook, eds. Kiley and McDonald, pp.
        174-81.

      Yossarian's actions make him "the perfect example
      of the 'new hero,' a man capable of restoring true
      sanity to the world," and, unlike Milo, shows
      "similarities to Christ."

189   Chanan, Gabriel. "The Plight of the Novelist." Cam-
      bridge Review, 26 April 1968, pp. 399-401.

      A discussion of the "molecular structure" of Catch-
      22, the non-spatial, non-chronological "net" or
      "web" of interrelationships that traps its victims
      without regard to time or space.

190   Cheuse, Alan. "Laughing on the Outside." Studies on
      the Left, 3 (Fall, 1963), 81-87.

      REPRINTED:
190a   A Catch-22 Casebook, eds. Kiley and McDonald, pp.
        86-93.

      Catch-22, beneath its "tough, flashy, comic mask,"
      is a "sentimental novel;" it fails as "coherent
      fiction" because the comic and tragic "intersect"
      and mar its otherwise superb surface with a "deep
      and destructive" flaw.

191   Cockburn, Alex. "Catch-22." New Left Review, 18 (1963),
      87-92.

      A long, generally praiseworthy review of Heller's
      satire, especially the "slick technique of paradox
      and dead-pan follow-through."

192   Cooperman, Stanley. <u>World War I and the American Novel</u>. Baltimore: Johns Hopkins, 1967, pp. 229-30.

A brief mention of <u>Catch-22</u> as a novel which "reacted savagely to any hint of the 'proving ground' of combat" through "comic antiheroism."

193   Davis, Douglas M. "Introduction: Notes on Black Humor," in <u>The World of Black Humor: An Introductory Anthology of Selections and Criticism</u>, ed. Davis. New York: E.P. Dutton, 1967, pp. 13-26.

A brief mention of <u>Catch-22</u>.

194   Davis, Robert Murray. "The Shrinking Garden and the New Exits: The Comic-Satiric Novel in the Twentieth Century." <u>Kansas Quarterly</u>, 1/3 (Summer, 1969), 5-16.

<u>Catch-22</u>'s Yossarian has reader empathy "far greater than in most previous works in the comic-satiric modes."

195   Day, Douglas. "Catch-22: A Manifesto for Anarchists." <u>Carolina Quarterly</u>, 15 (Summer, 1963), 86-92.

REPRINTED:
195a   <u>A Catch-22 Casebook</u>, eds. Kiley and McDonald, pp. 181-87.

Catch-22 is "derivative, poorly edited, repetitive and overlong," "a mixed bag, a hash." Yossarian, moreover, is an "anarchist" of the extreme sort: "no government, whether earthly or divine, is tolerable to him."

196   Denniston, Constance. "The American Romance Parody: A Study of Purdy's <u>Malcolm</u> and Heller's <u>Catch-22</u>." <u>Emporia State Research Studies</u>, 14/2 (1965), 42-59, 63-64.

REPRINTED:
196a   <u>A Catch-22 Casebook</u>, eds. Kiley and McDonald, pp. 51-57, in exerpt.
196b   <u>Critical Essays on Catch-22</u>, ed. James Nagel, pp. 64-77, in exerpt.

The novels of Purdy and Heller belong to the genre of the "romance parody," <u>Catch-22</u> being a parody of war. The structure of the book is a mixture of "startling clashes" whose "comic and tragic elements," and whose "two groups of characters and two plots" produce a powerful irony.

197   Dickstein, Morris. "Black Humor and History." Partisan
      Review, 43/2 (1976), 185-211.

      Catch-22 is one of those novels which "develop a
      striking and unusual sense of history that in the
      end tells us less about history than about the
      cultural tone of the period when they were written."
      Catch-22, Prof. Dickstein concludes, in its depiction
      of "callous inhumanity in a man-made world," is
      "the best novel of the sixties."

198   Dodd, Burwell. "Joseph Heller's Catch-22," in
      Approaches to the Novel, ed. John Colmer. Adelaide:
      Rigby, Ltd., 1967, pp. 71-78.

      Although the specific incidents of Catch-22 are often
      "improbable, and sometimes impossible," they are
      made credible by Heller's style; the novel, "pur-
      posefully confused," thus mirrors the "nightmare
      of chaos" in our world "as we have organized it."

199   Doskow, Minna. "The Night Journey in Catch-22."
      Twentieth Century Literature, 12 (January, 1967),
      186-93.

      REPRINTED:
199a A Critical Edition of Catch-22, ed. Robert M. Scotto,
      pp. 491-500.
199b A Catch-22 Casebook, eds. Kiley and McDonald, pp.
      166-74.
199c Critical Essays on Catch-22, ed. James Nagel, pp.
      155-63.

      After a close reading of the last four chapters,
      Prof. Doskow argues that Yossarian participates in
      "the archetypal pattern of the descent and renewal
      of the romance hero," and that his symbolic journey
      through Rome impels him into the "informed innocence"
      that culminates logically in his flight to Sweden.

200   Earney, Alan. "Catch-22." New York Times Book Review,
      28 April 1968, p. 49.

      Letter in response to Josh Greenfield's article
      of 3 March 1968.

201   Enck, John J. "John Barth: An Interview." Wisconsin
      Studies in Contemporary Literature, 6 (1965), 3-14.

      A brief mention of Heller, and Barth's favorable
      opinion of him.

202   Feldman, Burton. "Anatomy of Black Humor." Dissent,
      15 (1968), 158-60.

REPRINTED:
202a   The American Novel Since World War II, ed. Marcus
        Klein. Greenwich, Conn.: Fawcett, 1969, pp. 224-28.

        Brief mention of Catch-22.

203   French, Michael R. "The American Novel of the Sixties."
        Midwest Quarterly, 9/4 (July, 1968), 365-79.

        In a general essay, a reference to the "generic sym-
        bols" of Catch-22 (p. 370).

204   Friedman, Bruce J. "Those Clowns of Conscience." Book
        Week, 18 July 1965, pp. 2, 7.

        In a brief discussion of black humor, Heller's name
        is prominent.

205   Frost, Lucy. "Violence in the Eternal City: Catch-22
        as a Critique of American Culture." Meanjin Quarterly,
        30/4 (December, 1971), 447-53.

        A discussion of the ways in which Catch-22 is crit-
        ical of contemporary civilization: violence ("the
        fulcrum"), the interpenetration of military and
        civilian enterprise, the mis-use of the law. Catch-
        22, therefore, really "operates in 'peacetime' Amer-
        ica today."

206   Fussell, Paul. The Great War and Modern Memory. New
        York: Oxford University Press, 1975, pp. 34-35,
        307-09.

        Catch-22 is a good example of a novel about World
        War II which uses with great effect the "primal
        scene" of World War I fiction: the Snowden episode
        involves a "terribly injured man" comforted by a
        comrade "unaware of the real ghastliness of the
        friend's wound."

207   Galloway, David D. "Clown and Saint: The Hero in
        Current American Fiction." Critique, 7 (1965), 46-65.

        Yossarian is an example of the character of the
        comedian-redeemer so prevalent in contemporary
        American fiction (pp. 50-52).

208   Gaukroger, Doug. "Time Structure in Catch-22."
        Studies in Modern Fiction, 12/2 (1970), 70-85.

REPRINTED:
208a   A Catch-22 Casebook, eds. Kiley and McDonald, pp.
        132-44.
208b   Critical Essays on Catch-22, ed. James Nagel, pp.

89-101.

A refutation of Jan Solomon's thesis (see "The Structure of Joseph Heller's Catch-22"). Heller "does not need to develop an impossible time scheme to create a sense of absurdity and confusion in his novel; he achieves this effect better by obscuring and twisting a chronological structure which is both plausible and logical."

209 Gianakaris, C. J. "Tracking the Rebel in Literature." Topic, 9/18 (1969), 11-29.

A brief notation on Yossarian.

210 Gordon, Caroline and Jeanne Richardson. "Flies in Their Eyes? A Note on Joseph Heller's Catch-22." Southern Quarterly, 3 (Winter, 1967), 96-105.

REPRINTED:
210a Critical Essays on Catch-22, ed. James Nagel, pp. 117-24.

An unfavoravle comparison of the techniques of Heller and those of Lewis Carroll in Alice in Wonderland, though in both fantasies "the absurdities of life are contrasted with the way things ought to be or would be if the universe were governed by principles of formal logic."

211 Greenberg, Alvin. "The Novel of Disintegration: Paradoxical Impossibility in Contemporary Fiction." Wisconsin Studies in Contemporary Literature, 7/1 (Winter/Spring, 1966), 103-24.

Catch-22 is an excellent example of how, in our fiction, "chaos has usurped both the world outside and the individual within it"(pp. 115-17).

212 Greenberg, Alvin. "Choice: Ironic Alternatives to the World of the Contemporary American Novel," in American Dreams, American Nightmares, ed. Harry T. Moore. Southern Illinois University Press, 1970, pp. 175-87.

Yossarian's dilemma throughout Catch-22, and especially at the end of the novel, is discussed.

213 Greenfield, Josh. "22 Was Funnier Than 14." New York Times Book Review, 3 March 1968, pp. 49-51, 53.

REPRINTED:
213a A Catch-22 Casebook, eds. Kiley and McDonald, pp. 250-55.

A history of the writing of the novel as well as a discussion of its relevance to the problems of the sixties are presented informally.

214   Guerard, Albert J. "Saul Bellow and the Activists: On The Adventures of Augie March." Southern Review, NS 3 (1967), 582-96.

Catch-22 is referred to as an analogue.

215   Halio, Jay. "The Way It Is -- And Was." Southern Review, NS 6/1 (January, 1970), 250-62.

In a long review of many later novels, Catch-22 is referred to as a seminal example of the "paradoxical predicament" in contemporary fiction.

216   Harris, Charles B. Contemporary American Novelists of the Absurd. New Haven: College and University Press, 1971, pp. 33-50, passim.

A discussion of Catch-22 as a "radical protest novel" in which Heller "refuses to accept absurdity as an ontological fact," but rather views it as a result of power structures and bureaucracies impinging upon the individual. After the novel's characters, themes, devices and linguistic methods are treated, Prof. Harris concludes that "all that is traditional about Catch-22 is its protest," for with its publication "the Decade of the Absurd had begun."

217   Hasley, Louis. "Dramatic Tension in Catch-22." Midwest Quarterly, 15 (1974), 190-97.

The novel's tension "intensifies rather than alleviates" its irrationality, its "rapid, ecstatic, anguished shuttling" resisting the evil "suffered in this life by the insufficiently guilty."

218   Hassan, Ihab. Contemporary American Literature, 1945-1972: An Introduction. New York: Ungar, 1973, pp. 82-83.

Catch-22 is "a masterpiece of black comedy," a novel depicting "a disorder only Heller's imagination can contain, only his discontinuous form can render with integrity."

219   Hassan, Ihab. "The Dial and Recent American Fiction." CEA Critic, 29/1 (1966), 1, 3.

Brief mention of Catch-22.

220   Hassan, Ihab. "The Existential Novel." Massachusetts
       Review, 3/4 (Summer, 1962), 795-97.

       Catch-22 is included in the discussion.

221   Hassan, Ihab. "Laughter in the Dark: The New Voice in
       American Fiction." American Scholar, 33/4 (Autumn,
       1964), 636-38, 640.

       A brief mention of the comedy of Catch-22 which,
       "finally freed from the dark constant of the modern
       world, had suddenly overreached itself to the
       borders of chaos. But even chaos is sometimes apt."

222   Hauck, Richard Boyd. A Cheerful Nihilism: Confidence
       and The Absurd in American Humorous Fiction.
       Indiana University Press, 1971, pp. 11-12, 240.

       Catch-22 is representative of the theme explored in
       this book: the intimate relationship between the
       absurd and American humor.

223   Hicks, Granville. "Joseph Heller." Saturday Review,
       14 October 1961, p. 32.

       REPRINTED:
223a   Literary Horizons: A Quarter Century of American
       Fiction. New York University Press, 1970, pp.
       225-28.
223b   Critical Essays on Catch-22, ed. James Nagel, pp.
       11-12.

       Reprint of one of the earliest favorable reviews
       of Catch-22.

224   Hill, Hamlin. "Black Humor: Its Cause and Cure."
       Colorado Quarterly, 17/1 (Summer, 1968), 57-64.

       A brief mention of the Soldier in White episode in
       Catch-22 as an example of a passage "mixed with
       burlesque, fantasy, satire, and other comic modes."

225   Hoffman, Frederick J. The Mortal No. Princeton
       University Press, 1964, pp. 261-64.

       Catch-22 is a "wearisomely clever" exercise: the
       imbalance which has set in from the beginning -- a
       kind of nervous tic of giggles and laughs, like a
       punster stammering -- succeeds in holding off the
       threat of meaning."

226   Hunt, John W. "Comic Escape and Anti-Vision: The
       Novels of Joseph Heller and Thomas Pynchon," in
       Adversity and Grace: Studies in Recent American

Literature, ed. Nathan A. Scott. University of
Chicago Press, 1968, pp. 87-112.

REPRINTED:
226a   A Catch-22 Casebook, eds. Kiley and McDonald, pp.
        242-47, in exerpt.
226b   Critical Essays on Catch-22, ed. James Nagel, pp.
        125-30, in exerpt.

Hunt discusses Catch-22 as a "novel of saturation,"
an inclusive comic structure wherein "fantasy becomes the norm."

227   Janoff, Bruce. "Black Humor, Existentialism, and
        Absurdity: A Generic Confusion." Arkansas Quarterly,
        30 (1974), 293-304.

In an exploratory essay, Catch-22 is cited.

228   Karl, Frederick R. "Joseph Heller's Catch-22: Only
        Fools Walk in Darkness," in Contemporary American
        Novelists, ed. Harry T. Moore. Southern Illinois
        University Press, 1964, pp. 132-42.

REPRINTED:
228a   A Critical Edition of Catch-22, ed. Robert M. Scotto,
        pp. 481-88.
228b   A Catch-22 Casebook, eds. Kiley and McDonald, pp.
        159-65.

An exploration of the "appealing nihilism" of Catch-
22, its "affirmations" "couched in terms of pain and
cynical laughter." The discussion of the novel's
satire is implemented by a brief history of Heller's
manuscript changes before publication.

229   Kazin, Alfred. "The War Novel: From Mailer to Vonne-
        gut." Saturday Review, 6 February 1971, pp. 13-15,
        36.

REPRINTED:
229a   The Bright Book of Life. Boston: Atlantic, Little,
        Brown, 1973, pp. 82-86.
229b   A Critical Edition of Catch-22, ed. Robert M. Scotto,
        pp. 488-91, in exerpt.

Catch-22 is discussed as a war novel written against
the grain, for Heller "combines the bitterness of
a total pacifist with the mocking pseudo-rationality
of traditional Jewish humor."

230   Kennard, Jean. "Joseph Heller: At War with Absurdity."
        Mosaic, 4/3 (Spring, 1971), 75-87.

REPRINTED:

230a   A Critical Edition of Catch-22, ed. Robert Scotto, pp. 526-41.

230b   A Catch-22 Casebook, eds. Kiley and McDonald, pp. 255-69.

230c   Number and Nightmare: Forms of Fantasy in Contemporary Fiction. Hamden, Conn.: Archon, 1975, pp. 41-56.

Although Catch-22 is "absurd" in the existential sense, Heller's techniques do not describe, but rather "dramatize" the human condition. Yossarian's sense of futility is realized through several devices, discussed at length, and Heller's unique comic style.

231   Klein, Marcus. "Introduction" to The American Novel Since World War II. Greenwich, Conn.: Fawcett, 1969, pp. 9-23.

Catch-22 is mentioned in this survey.

232   Kort, Wesley. Shriven Selves: Religious Problems in Recent American Fiction. Philadelphia: Fortress Press, 1972, p. 61.

The debate on religion in Catch-22 is mentioned.

233   Kostelanetz, Richard. "American Fiction of the Sixties," in On Contemporary Literature. Expanded Edition. New York: Avon, 1969, p. 639.

A brief discussion of Catch-22 as a prototypical "absurd" novel.

234   Kostelanetz, Richard. "Dada and the Future of Fiction." Works, 1/3 (1968), 58-66.

In a study of the methods of Dada, Catch-22 is noted as containing "qualities reminiscent of Dada"(p. 63).

235   Kostelanetz, Richard. "The New American Fiction," in New American Arts. New York: Horizon, 1965, pp. 212-214.

Catch-22 is a novel with "such a needlessly wild discrepancy in the style of representation, running from naturalism through surrealism, from the grotesque to parody and comic satire to symbolic fantasy" that "Heller's literary future remains unpredictable."

236   Kostelanetz, Richard. "The Point Is That Life Doesn't Have Any Point." New York Times Book Review, 6 June 1965, p. 3.

REPRINTED:
236a   "The American Absurd Novel (1965)," in The World
        of Black Humor: An Introductory Anthology of
        Selections and Criticisms, ed. Douglas M. Davis.
        New York: E. P. Dutton, 1967, pp. 306-313.

        A brief response to the absurdity of Catch-22.

237   Kubly, Herbert. "The Vanishing Novel." Saturday
        Review, 2 May 1964, pp. 12-15, 26.

        Catch-22 is considered one of the good new novels
        which exist outside of the mainstream of publish-
        ing. One of the reasons that fewer novels are pub-
        lished in proportion to other books in today's
        market is that the traditional novel is no longer
        being written and the tradition is, consequently,
        not enriched.

238   Le Clair, Thomas. "Death and Black Humor." Critique,
        17/1 (1975), 5-40.

        Catch-22 "illustrates . . . that affirmation for the
        writer who knows and presents death's potency is
        desired but difficult to achieve," and that Some-
        thing Happened is "a profound study of domestic
        life and the ramifications of death anxiety in our
        time," thus extending "the personal (and social)
        insights of Catch-22"(pp. 14-17).

239   Lehan, Richard and Jerry Patch. "Catch-22: The Making
        of a Novel." Minnesota Review, 7 (1967), 238-44.

        REPRINTED:
239a   A Dangerous Crossing. Carbondale: Southern Illinois
        University Press, 1973, pp. 163-72.
239b   Critical Essays on Catch-22, ed. James Nagel, pp.
        37-44.

        The first part of the essay is concerned with bureau-
        cratic absurdity in the novel; the second part deals
        with a welter of autobiographical detail as related
        by a friend of Mr. Heller's, and which he has pub-
        lically rejected.

240   Levine, Paul. "The Intemperate Zone: The Climate of
        Contemporary American Fiction." Massachusetts Re-
        view, 8/2 (Spring, 1967), 505-23.

        The "distress" we feel behind the "affluence" of
        contemporary America is reflected in our fiction,
        Catch-22 but one of the many illustrations (p. 519).

241   Levine, Paul. "The Politics of Alienation." Mosaic,

2/1 (Fall, 1968), 3-17.

Catch-22 is a "novel about World War Two from the vantage point of Vietnam, which, with its increasing bombing levels, its destruction of a city 'in order to save it,' and its institutionalized Credibility Gap, is the world of Catch-22"(pp. 9-12).

242   Lewis, R. W. B. Trials of the Word. Yale University Press, 1965, pp. 226-27.

A brief discussion of the black humor of Catch-22.

243   Littlejohn, David. "The Anti-Realists." Daedalus, 92/2 (Spring, 1963), 250-64.

In a discussion of the "novel of fantasy, illogicality and absurdity," of "fiction of the dreaming, subconscious self," Catch-22 is described as the "best example" for "the entire case for anti-realism" in a single novel (pp. 258-59).

244   Loukides, Paul. "The Radical Vision." Michigan Academician, 5 (1973), 497-503.

Catch-22 is mentioned as a radical novel.

245   Loukides, Paul. "Some Notes on the Novel of the Absurd." CEA Critic, 30/4 (1968), 8, 13.

A brief mention of Catch-22.

246   Mailer, Norman. "Some Children of the Goddess." Esquire, July, 1963, pp. 63-69.

REPRINTED:
246a   Contemporary American Novelists, ed. Harry T. Moore. Southern Illinois University Press, 1964, pp. 3-31.

An idiosyncratic response to Catch-22 as "original" yet "maddening." "If I were a major critic, it would be a virtuoso performance to write a definitive piece on Catch-22. It would take ten thousand words or more." He concludes: "Heller may yet become Gogol"(pp. 66-67).

247   Martine, James J. "The Courage To Defy," in Critical Essays on Catch-22, ed. James Nagel, pp. 142-49.

After a brief analysis of some of Heller's early stories, Catch-22's "discursive" quality and narrow vision are explained as the novel's two major weaknesses; the result is not a great novel, but "an interesting and attractive piece of work."

248   McDonald, James L. "I See Everything Twice: The
Structure of Joseph Heller's Catch-22." University
Review, 34 (Spring, 1968), 175-80.

REPRINTED:
248a   A Catch-22 Casebook, eds. Kiley and McDonald, pp.
102-08.

Déjà vu dominates the non-chronological sequence of
events. The novel's construction and its thematic
patterns, both analyzed carefully, give the reader
the feeling of seeing every event at least twice.

249   McDonald, Walter R. "He Took Off: Yossarian and the
Different Drummer." CEA Critic, 36 (1973), 14-16.

A note on Yossarian's heroism, against the grain,
within the American tradition.

250   McDonald, Walter R. "Look Back in Horror: The Functional Comedy of Catch-22." CEA Critic, 35/2 (January,
1973), 18-21.

A brief discussion of the horror in Catch-22 which
concludes: "Heller's black, savage humor turns the
world on end in order to arouse a jaded audience.
The line is surrealistically thin, he seems to say,
between fantasy and reality."

251   McK. Henry, G. B. "Significant Corn: Catch-22." Mel-
bourne Critical Review, 9 (1966), 133-44.

REPRINTED:
251a   A Catch-22 Casebook, eds. Kiley and McDonald, pp.
187-201.

Catch-22 is a "cinematic novel" whose strength is
in its richness and its variety, but which is too
compromised to contain "the full implications of
tragedy."

252   McNamara, Eugene. "The Absurd Style in Contemporary
American Literature." Humanities Association
Bulletin, 19/1 (Winter, 1968), 44-49.

The absurd style, of which Catch-22 is representative, may have reached its limit and become self-
parody.

253   Mellard, James M. "Catch-22: Déjà Vu and the Labyrinth of Memory." Bucknell Review, 16 (May, 1968),
29-44.

REPRINTED:

253a   A Critical Edition of Catch-22, ed. Robert M. Scotto,
       pp. 512-25.
253b   A Catch-22 Casebook, eds. Kiley and McDonald, pp.
       109-121.

       Déjà vu "suggests something of the delusive exper-
       ience, hallucinatory quality, and disjunctive
       expression of reality in Catch-22." Seeing things
       twice expands the novel into a statement of "a
       universal myth, the myth of the journey into the
       underworld, the labyrinth, the heart of darkness."

254   Miller, James E. Quests Surd and Absurd: Essays in
       American Literature. University of Chicago Press,
       1967, pp. 12-13, 15-17, 24-25.

       A brief study of Catch-22 as a classic example of
       contemporary absurdist literature.

255   Miller, Wayne Charles. An Armed America, Its Face In
       Fiction: A History of the American Military Novel.
       New York University Press, 1970, pp. 205-43.

       In a chapter entitled "Joseph Heller's Catch-22:
       Satire Sums Up A Tradition," Yossarian's "ultimate-
       ly achieved value system" is discussed. By going
       beyond the war novel, and by rejecting "commit-
       ments to the various faiths of his culture,"
       Heller has summed up a tradition by subsuming it.

256   Milne, Victor J. "Heller's 'Bologniad': A Theological
       Perspective on Catch-22." Critique, 12/2 (1970),
       50-69.

       REPRINTED:
256a   A Catch-22 Casebook, eds. Kiley and McDonald, pp.
       58-73.

       A study of the "mock-epic form" Heller uses to
       dramatize the clash between "a Christian ethic of
       universal benevolence" exemplified by Yossarian,
       and "the competitive ethic" of the novel's villains.

257   Monk, Donald. "An Experiment in Therapy: A Study of
       Catch-22." London Review, 2 (Autumn, 1967), 12-19.

       REPRINTED:
257a   A Catch-22 Casebook, eds. Kiley and McDonald, pp.
       212-220.

       Heller's "concentration of action and hallucination"
       is a form of therapy against horror: since "a
       sublimation into fantasy is the necessary end of
       the novel," we find consolation in it because it

is "impossible."

258   Muste, John H. "Better to Die Laughing: The War Novels
      of Joseph Heller and John Ashmead." Critique, 5/2
      (Fall, 1962), 16-27.

      Both Heller and Ashmead draw "heavily upon a less
      popular tradition in which the military experience
      is treated as essentially humorous." Both rely
      heavily on stock characters, both juxtapose humor
      and bloodshed, and both are "set apart from tra-
      ditional satire" in their "preoccupation with death."

259   Nagel, James. "Introduction," to Critical Essays on
      Catch-22, pp. 1-7.

      A general survey of the critical response to the
      novel, Heller's short fiction, and a breakdown of
      the various approaches to the text of Catch-22.

260   Nagel, James. "Two Brief Manuscript Sketches:
      Heller's Catch-22." Modern Fiction Studies, 20
      (Summer, 1974), 221-24.

      An analysis of the changes in Heller's conception
      of Catch-22 as it evolved based upon Heller's
      notes for what later became the hospital scene
      ("Catch-18" and then Chapter I, "The Texan"). In
      the process of revision all of the original ethnic
      qualities of the characters (in one version Yossar-
      ian is Jewish) are erased.

261   Nagel, James. "Yossarian, The Old Man, and the End-
      ing of Catch-22," in Critical Essays on Catch-22,
      pp. 164-74.

      An analysis of the affinity of Yossarian to the
      old man in the Roman whorehouse, "a projection
      of what he is becoming." At the end of the novel,
      therefore, he is the only major character "who
      learns from experience."

262   Nelson, Gerald B. Ten Versions of America. New York:
      Knopf, 1972, pp. 165-82.

      A general discussion of the plot and themes of
      Catch-22, with special emphasis on the isolation
      of the characters and the contrast between Yossar-
      ian and Minderbinder.

263   Nelson, Thomas Allen. "Theme and Structure in Catch-22."
      Renascence, 23/4 (Summer, 1971), 178-82.

      A study of the "cyclical pattern of action which

complements the multifarious ideas and issues associated with the theme of responsibility."

264   Oglesby, Carl. "The Deserters: The Contemporary Defeat of Fiction." Motive, 28 (February, 1968), 14-24.

A brief discussion of Catch-22 as an example of a contemporary novel whose protagonist is an anti-hero.

265   Olderman, Raymond Michael. Beyond the Waste Land: The American Novel in the Nieteen-Sixties. Yale University Press, 1972, pp. 94-114.

Catch-22 deals with the "one real terror that haunts the novel of the sixties": institutionalization. The novel's "waste land," therefore, is the military-economic complex wherein justice is impossible, and through which Yossarian emerges as the weary knight of the grail who "departs not to affirm life but to survive as a dispossessed man."

266   Orr, Richard W. "Flat Characters in Catch-22." Notes on Contemporary Literature, 1/1 (1971), 4.

A brief note on the allegorical figures in the novel.

267   Pease, Donald. "Catch-22." Casette lecture. Florida: Everett/Edwards.

268   Pinsker, Sanford. "Heller's Catch-22: The Protest of a Puer Eternis." Critique, 7/2 (Winter, 1964/65), 150-62.

Yossarian, though he "adopts the attitude of a perennial innocent," is still a "protest figure" fitting comfortably in the American tradition. Since Catch-22 lacks "philosophical content," its "style" is responsible for its popularity.

269   Podhoretz, Norman. Doings and Undoings. New York: Farrar, Straus, 1964, pp. 228-35.

In a chapter entitled "The Best Catch There Is," the novel's success is attributed to Heller's ability to show "what insanity looks like" rather than explaining "how it came about." Like Donleavy's Ginger Man, Yossarian is an idealist exposing "pretenses."

270   Protherough, Robert. "The Sanity of Catch-22." Human World, 3 (May, 1971), 59-70.

REPRINTED:
270a   A Critical Edition of Catch-22, ed. Robert M. Scotto,

pp. 541-44, in exerpt.
270b   A Catch-22 Casebook, eds. Kiley and McDonald, pp.
        201-12.

        An analysis of Heller's satiric devices, very
        thoroughly done, all of which turn upon a sudden
        reversal, and all of which are presented humor-
        ously at the beginning of Catch-22 but more serious-
        ly later in the book.

271   Ramsey, Vance. "From Here to Absurdity: Heller's
        Catch-22," in Seven Contemporary Authors, ed.
        Thomas B. Whitbread. University of Texas Press,
        1966, pp. 97-118.

        REPRINTED:
271a   A Catch-22 Casebook, eds. Kiley and McDonald, pp.
        221-36.

        The question of madness and sanity is central to
        the technique of Catch-22, and Yossarian's aggressive
        "antiheroism" is a challenge to the absurd: "he
        constantly rejects attempts to make him over in
        terms of any ideal."

272   "A Review: Catch-22." Daedalus, 92 (Winter, 1963),
        155-65.

        REPRINTED:
272a   The American Reading Public: What It Reads, Why It
        Reads, ed. Roger H. Smith. New York: Bowker, 1963,
        pp. 234-47.
272b   A Catch-22 Casebook, eds. Kiley and McDonald, pp.
        27-39.
272c   Critical Essays on Catch-22, ed. James Nagel, pp.
        21-33, mistakenly attributed to Roger H. Smith.

        To date still the most virulent argument against
        the merits of Catch-22 yet printed. The anonymous
        reviewer feels, among other things, that the novel
        is "worthless," and that Heller "cannot write."

273   Richter, D. H. Fable's End: Completeness and Closure
        in Rhetorical Fiction. University of Chicago Press,
        1974, pp. 136-65.

        In a chapter entitled "The Achievement of Shape in
        the Twentieth Century Fable" Catch-22 is highly
        praised: "Its form represents an achievement towards
        which contemporary rhetorical fiction has been
        groping." The novel's "closure" is Yossarian's re-
        volt: "utopia, no matter how far out of reach, is
        a meaningful ideal for which man may strive."

274   Ritter, Jesse. "Fearful Comedy: Catch-22 as Avatar
       of the Social Surrealist Novel," in A Catch-22
       Casebook, eds. Kiley and McDonald, pp. 73-86.

       The social surrealist novel -- "a mixture of picar-
       esque, romance-parody, and anatomy" -- contains
       "elements of surrealism, black humor, the grotesque
       and tragicomedy, the Absurd, apocalyptic visions,
       and a semi-mythic antiherc." Catch-22 is a radical
       novel in which "irony is raised to the level of
       structure."

275   Ritter, Jesse. "What Manner of Men Are These," in
       Critical Essays on Catch-22, ed. James Nagel, pp.
       45-56.

       The struggles within Catch-22 are presented through
       two character types of Jonsonian "humors." The
       aggressors, in whom Heller embodies "a rigorous
       critique of capitalism," inevitably drive the
       victims to a separate peace.

276   Rubin, Louis D. "The Curious Death of the Novel: Or,
       What To Do About Tired Literary Critics." Kenyon
       Review, 28 (1966), 305-25.

       REPRINTED:
276a   The Curious Death of the Novel: Essays in American
       Literature. Louisiana State University Press,
       1967, pp. 3-23.

       Brief mention of Heller as an example of the strength
       of the contemporary novel in spite of rumors to the
       contrary.

277   Ryan, Marjorie. "Four Contemporary Satires and the
       Problem of Norms." Satire Newsletter, 6/2 (Spring,
       1969), 40-46.

       A discussion of how Catch-22 destroys old as well
       as develops new satiric forms (pp. 42-43): "The
       ultimate norm is that war is madness, and peace
       sanity."

278   Scammell, W. "Letter in Reply to Mr. Wain." Critical
       Quarterly, 5 (Autumn, 1963), 273-74.

       REPRINTED:
278a   A Catch-22 Casebook, eds. Kiley and McDonald, pp.
       49-50.

       An argument against Wain's qualified praise (see
       "A New Novel About Old Troubles") of Catch-22, which
       Mr. Scammell thinks is not "of lasting worth" because

Heller switches between "the 'fantastic' and the 'naturalistic' mode [sic], and so destroys both the tone and the unity of the narrative."

279   Scholes, Robert. "'Mithridates, he died old': Black Humor and Kurt Vonnegut, Jr." in The Sounder Few: Essays From The Hollins Critic, eds. R. H. W. Dillard, et. al. Athens, Georgia, 1971, pp. 172-85.

Catch-22 figures prominently in an attempt to fix Vonnegut's peculiar humor.

280   Schopf, William. "Blindfolded and Backwards: Promethean and Bemushroomed Heroism in One Flew Over The Cuckoo's Nest and Catch-22." Bulletin of the Rocky Mountain Language Association, 26 (1972), 89-97.

A comparison of the protagonists of the two novels, MacMurphy and Yossarian, especially in their suffering and redemptive value.

281   Schulz, Max F. "Pop, Op, and Black Humor: The Aesthetics of Anxiety." College English, 30/3 (December, 1968), 230-41.

REPRINTED:
281a   Black Humor Fiction of the Sixties: A Pluralistic Definition of Man and His World. Athens, Ohio: Ohio University Press, 1973, pp. 22-23, 91-92, 141-42, passim.

A brief discussion of Colonel Cathcart as the man of "angst" -- the "small, aspiring, flattened, big, weak Massenmensch of our century." Catch-22 also illustrates the "disquieted average" in contemporary fiction.

282   Scotto, Robert M. "Introduction" to A Critical Edition of Catch-22. New York: Delta, 1973, pp. v-ix.

An argument for the novel's popularity based upon its merits rather than its popularity. An analysis of the last quarter of Catch-22 attempts to show that a technical as well as thematic change occurs, thus making one of the most significant experiments in contemporary fiction.

283   Shapiro, Stephen A. "The Ambivalent Animal: Man in the Contemporary British and American Novel." Centennial Review, 12/1 (1968), 1-22.

A brief attack on the "meretricious qualities" of Catch-22: "The creator of Yossarian not only sentimentalizes human nature; he avoids the terrible

nature of the conflict he is supposedly dealing
with."

284   Skerrett, Joseph Taylor, Jr. "Dostoievsky, Nathanael
       West, and Some Contemporary American Fiction."
       University of Dayton Review, 4/1 (1967), 23-36.

       Catch-22 is mentioned briefly.

285   Sniderman, Stephen L. "'It Was All Yossarian's Fault':
       Power and Responsibility in Catch-22." Twentieth
       Century Literature, 19/4 (October, 1973), 251-58.

       An argument that, "in the fictional sense,"
       Yossarian "is responsible for nearly every signifi-
       cant event mentioned in the novel." His inability
       to prevent tragedy, therefore, makes him "the real
       culprit" in light of Heller's position exalting
       the individual.

286   Solomon, Eric. "From Christ in Flanders to Catch-22:
       An Approach to War Fiction." Texas Studies in
       Literature and Language, 11/1 (Spring, 1969), 851-66.

       REPRINTED:
286a   A Catch-22 Casebook, eds. Kiley and McDonald, pp.
          94-101.

       Catch-22 "culminates a tradition of bitterly ironic
       war fiction," but it differs from its predecessors
       in its "corruscating humor" and its despair.

287   Solomon, Jan. "The Structure of Heller's Catch-22."
       Critique, 9/2 (1967), 46-57.

       REPRINTED:
287a   A Critical Edition of Catch-22, ed. Robert M. Scotto,
          pp. 510-11.
287b   A Catch-22 Casebook, eds. Kiley and McDonald, pp.
          122-32.
287c   Critical Essays on Catch-22, ed. James Nagel, pp.
          78-88.

       The form of Catch-22 is "carefully constructed to
       support the pervasive theme of absurdity," especial-
       ly its chronology. While the major part of the novel
       focuses on Yossarian moving forward and back in time,
       a "counter-motion" is the history of Milo, who
       moves "directly" from success to success. The two
       movements are "irreconcilable," and thus enforce
       the theme of "the repudiation of the business
       ethic."

288   Standiford, Les. "Novels into Film: Catch-22 as Water-

shed." Southern Humanities Review, 8 (Winter, 1974), 19-25.

A generally favorable reception of Mike Nichols' film because it avoids the pitfalls of adapting a complex text and concentrates on "a tight, somber progression of scenes moving to Yossarian's moment of decision."

289   Stark, Howard J. "The Anatomy of Catch-22," in A Catch-22 Casebook, eds. Kiley and McDonald, pp. 145-58.

A discussion of Heller's "juxtaposition of incongruities," "renunciation of time," "failure of language," "the use of the ludicrous and the illogical," and "the depiction of deep-seated feelings of frustration and anguish." Catch-22's scenes and images are also analyzed.

290   Stark, Howard J. "Catch-22: The Ultimate Irony," in Critical Essays on Catch-22, ed. James Nagel, pp. 130-41.

Yossarian's "leap" at the end is a "paridigm" for the entire novel. Since "the adherence to a solid moral position is useless," the ultimate irony of Catch-22 is that one will be destroyed whether he adapts or not.

291   Stern, J. P. "War and the Comic Muse: The Good Soldier Schweik and Catch-22." Comparative Literature, 20 (Summer, 1968), 193-216.

Of the two novels discussed, Catch-22 is "a much more highly-wrought work," especially in the scenes involving the absurd conflict between military machine and individual. He concludes: "the principle of self-protection" dominates both novels.

292   Tanner, Tony. "The Great American Nightmare." Spectator, 29 April 1966, pp. 530-31.

Mention of Catch-22 in a review of Schneck's The Nightclerk.

293   Tanner, Tony. "A Mode of Motion," in City of Words. New York: Harper and Row, 1971, pp. 72-84.

An analysis of dark comedy in Catch-22 with special emphasis on the characters who can survive in the "intolerable" world, and those who work against "controlled environment." The "significant" ending is carefully delineated.

294   Thomas, W. K. "The Mythic Dimension of Catch-22."
       Texas Studies in Literature and Language, 15/1
       (Spring, 1973), 189-98.

       A discussion of Heller's use of myth in his char-
       acterizations of Chief White Halfoat, Orr, Yossar-
       ian, Aarfy, Nately's whore, and how it justifies
       the "swing up" at the end of the novel.

295   Thomas, W. K. "'What Difference Does It Make?' Logic
       in Catch-22." Dalhousie Review, 50/4 (Winter, 1970/
       71), 488-95.

       Heller's "distinction between form and substance"
       and his "faulty logic" both "amuse" as well as
       "look at ideas in a new light" in order to "expose
       some of the irrationality that is at the center of
       many things."

296   Trachtenberg, Stanley. "Counterhumor: Comedy in
       Contemporary American Fiction." Georgia Review,
       27/1 (Spring, 1973), 33-48.

       Catch-22 is noted briefly (pp. 36-37).

297   Vos, Melvin. For God's Sake Laugh! Richmond: John
       Knox, 1967, pp. 53-58.

       REPRINTED:
297a   A Catch-22 Casebook, eds. Kiley and McDonald, pp.
       247-50.

       A discussion of the humor in Catch-22. Heller, the
       satirist, is considered one of the "clowns of
       conscience."

298   Wain, John. "A New Novel About Old Troubles." Critical
       Quarterly, 5 (Summer, 1963), 168-73.

       REPRINTED:
298a   A Catch-22 Casebook, eds. Kiley and McDonald, pp.
       43-49.

       The satire of Catch-22 is treated: its "one serious
       flaw" is its "central evasiveness," yet it never-
       theless portrays a world gone wrong very poignantly.
       Yossarian "is the hero of every modern novel."

299   Walden, Daniel. "'Therefore Choose Life': A Jewish
       Interpretation of Heller's Catch-22," in Critical
       Essays on Catch-22, ed. James Nagel, pp. 57-63.

       A brief study which offers the view that Heller
       "may have gone beyond the commonplace to create

an anti-hero to whom the older values were remembered
in a world without values."

300 Waldmeir, Joseph J. "Only an Occasional Rutabaga:
American Fiction Since 1945." Modern Fiction Studies,
15/4 (Winter, 1969/70), 467-81.

A brief mention of Catch-22.

301 Waldmeir, Joseph J. "Two Novelists of the Absurd:
Heller and Kesey." Wisconsin Studies in Contemporary
Literature, 5/3 (Autumn, 1964), 192-204.

REPRINTED:
301a American Novels of the Second World War. The Hague:
Mouton, 1969, pp. 160-65.
301b Ken Kesey's One Flew Over the Cuckoo's Nest: Text
Criticism, ed. John C. Pratt. New York: Viking,
1973, pp. 401-18.
301c Critical Essays on Catch-22, ed. James Nagel, pp.
150-54, in exerpt.

One Flew Over the Cuckoo's Nest is a far better
"absurdist" novel than Catch-22 because it is tighter,
more carefully controlled. Heller's vision is "dis-
concerting," "plotless," "chaotic," and thus less
successful in capturing the feel of a world gone
mad.

302 Walters, Raymond, Jr. "Catch Cult." New York Times
Book Review, 9 September 1962, p. 8.

A brief history of Catch-22's reception and
popularity.

303 Way, Brian. "Formal Experiment and Social Discontent"
Joseph Heller's Catch-22." Journal of American
Studies, 2/2 (October, 1968), 253-70.

A long essay which analyzes the "power to transform
American literature, to re-invigorate a fiction"
that Catch-22 possesses because it is both a radical
protest novel in content and a "new" absurd novel
in technique at the same time.

304 Weatherby, W. J. "The Joy Catcher." Guardian, 20 November 1962, p. 7.

A recollection of a discussion with Heller in which
he admitted his respect for Celine, Waugh, Nabokov.

305 West, Paul. The Modern Novel. London: Hutchinson, 1963,
pp. 313-15.

A brief introduction of Catch-22 to the British.

306   Widmer, Kingsley. The Literary Rebel. Carbondale:
      Southern Illinois University Press, 1965, pp. 103, 235.

      Heller is briefly referred to as an example of a
      "popular rebel writer."

307   Wincelberg, Shimon. "A Deadly Serious Lunacy." New
      Leader, 14 May 1962, pp. 26-27.

      REPRINTED:
307a On Contemporary Literature, ed. Richard Kostelanetz.
      New York: Avon, 1964, pp. 388-91.

      A reprint of a favorable review.

                        iii. Pynchon

                        a. General

308   Allen, Mary. The Necessary Blankness: Women in Major
      American Fiction of the Sixties. University of
      Illinois Press, 1976, pp. 37-51.

      A discussion of women in Pynchon's novels: "He
      stands out among contemporary writers in develop-
      ing the most extensive mythic view of women in V."
      In Lot 49, Oedipa is "a sympathetic portrayal of
      woman as a forsaken mass," a "lonely consumer,"
      a "pawn."

309   Dickstein, Morris. "Black Humor and History." Partisan
      Review, 43/2 (1976), 185-211.

      Lot 49, especially, and V. "develop a striking and
      unusual sense of history that in the end tells us
      less about history than about the cultural tone of
      the period when they were written." Lot 49, he con-
      cludes, is a novel "both impressively somber in tone
      and yet amazingly conditional and tentative in sub-
      stance," and a "revelation."

310   Harris, Charles B. Contemporary American Novelists of
      the Absurd. New Haven: College and University Press,
      1971, pp. 76-99.

      A discussion of "entropy" in Pynchon's early fiction,
      history in V. (pp. 79-93), communications in Lot 49
      (pp. 93-99). Pynchon's is an art of "complex fabric."

311   Hassan, Ihab. Contemporary American Literature, 1945-

1972: An Introduction. New York: Ungar, 1973, pp. 84-85.

A brief discussion of Pynchon, who pushes the novel "farther toward auto-destruction and pessimistic play" than any of his contemporaries," an "exotic Joycean" and "camp anti-novelist."

312   Hendin, Josephine. "What Is Thomas Pynchon Telling Us?" *Harper's,* March, 1975, pp. 82-92.

A long, idiosyncratic piece on *V.* and *Gravity's Rainbow* which offers Pynchon as "the evil genius of our time," identified, at the close, with the "antichrist," the "devil" and "death," the writer who has "offered up his own destructiveness to illuminate yours."

313   Henkle, Roger B. "Pynchon's Tapestries on the Western World." *Modern Fiction Studies,* 17/2 (Summer, 1971), 207-20.

The "romantic epic" is seen as appropriate to Pynchon's objectives in *V.* and *Lot 49*: "a loose structure, highly fictionalized reinterpretation of a past culture, and an emphasis on literary invention almost for its own sake." His affinity to Nabokov is also discussed.

314   Hunt, John W. "Comic Escape and Anti-Vision: The Novels of Joseph Heller and Thomas Pynchon," in *Adversity and Grace,* ed. Nathan Scott, Jr. University of Chicago Press, 1968, pp. 87-112.

A discussion of Pynchon's absurd techniques and characters, especially the "multiple connections" which create "discontinuity" and "obscurity," but which also make life bearable.

315   Kazin, Alfred. *The Bright Book of Life.* Boston: Atlantic, Little, Brown, 1973, pp. 275-80.

A brief discussion of *V.* and *Lot 49* as novels whose "protagonist is History itself," and whose key is "a felt mystery, a communicable unsolidity, to our human affairs."

316   Klinkowitz, Jerome. *Literary Disruptions: The Making of a Post-Contemporary American Fiction.* Urbana: University of Illinois Press, 1975, pp. 11-15.

A brief discussion of Pynchon as "a member of the school of Exhaustion. His techniques do not serve an attempt to create stable fictions, but as a commentary on themselves."

317 Kostelanetz, Richard. "American Fiction of the Sixties," in On Contemporary Literature. Expanded
Edition. New York: Avon, 1969, pp. 634-52.

A brief discussion of V. and Lot 49 (pp. 640, 650-
51) in which the former is highly praised.

318 Krafft, John M. "Anarcho-Romanticism and the Meta-
physics of Counterforce: Alex Comfort and Thomas
Pynchon." Paunch, 40/41 (April, 1975), 78-107.

An attempt to correlate Pynchon's vision of the
decline of the west with Comfort's social criticism,
especially insofar as the "victimization" of in-
dividuals and the "death-orientation" of civilization are concerned.

319 Levine, George and David Leverenz. "Introduction:
Mindful Pleasures." Twentieth Century Literature,
21/2 (May, 1975), iii-v.

REPRINTED:
319a Mindful Pleasures: Essays on Thomas Pynchon. Boston:
Little, Brown, 1976, pp. 3-11.

A brief overview of the special Pynchon number of
Twentieth Century Literature, expanded in the
collection of essays to include an overview of
Pynchon criticism in general.

320 Levine, George. "Risking the Moment: Anarchy and
Possibility in Pynchon's Fiction," in Mindful
Pleasures, eds. Levine and Leverenz, pp. 113-36.

An analysis of the virtuosity of Pynchon's prose,
which is "most disorienting and testing" in "its
almost sullen resistance to judging the various
horrors it coldly narrates." The Pynchon character
is imagined "as participating in the energies of
the world created around it."

321 McConnell, Frank D. "Thomas Pynchon," in Contemporary
Novelists, ed. James Vinson. New York, 1972, pp.
1033-36.

A discussion of "the most uncompromising and cour-
ageous of the analysts of our psychic debilities"
who tells his "sewer stories" "against the darkness,
that we might better, by talking aloud, see each
other."

322 Olderman, Raymond M. Beyond the Waste Land: The

American Novel in the Nineteen-Sixties. New Haven:
Yale University Press, 1972, pp. 123-49.

A discussion of the "three realms" of V. (pp. 123-
44): "the private, the public-political, and what
might be called the metaphysical." A "note" on
Lot 49 (pp. 144-49) develops Pynchon's concept of
conspiracy.

323   Poirier, Richard. "Cook's Tour." New York Review of
       Books, 1/2 (1963), 32.

       REPRINTED:
323a   The Performing Self. New York: Oxford University
       Press, 1971, pp. 23-26.

       A brief discussion of Pynchon's plots. "The knotty
       entanglements" are meant to "testify to waste,"
       for there is implied "the mad belief that some
       plot can ultimately take over the world."

324   Poirier, Richard. "The Importance of Pynchon."
       Twentieth Century Literature, 21/2 (May, 1975), 151-
       62.

       REPRINTED:
324a   Mindful Pleasures, ed. Levine and Leverenz, pp. 15-29.

       An introduction to the difficulty of establishing
       Pynchon's audience, the problems of his texts, his
       "distinctly American vision." Pynchon might be
       composing "encoded warnings," for he is "a great
       novelist of betrayal."

325   Schulz, Max F. "The Unconfirmed Thesis: Kurt Vonnegut,
       Black Humor, and Contemporary Art." Critique, 12/3
       (1971), 5-28.

       A brief discussion of V. and Lot 49 (pp. 25-27) and
       their "sense of imminent revelation," especially
       within the context of other works of black humor.

326   Shorris, Earl. "The Worldly Palimpsest of Thomas
       Pynchon." Harper's, June, 1973, pp. 78-80, 83.

       A wholly negative survey of the three novels,
       attacking their solipsism, nihilism, prose, and
       "hopeless and haughty satire." "For all of the
       inventions, Mr. Pynchon's work lacks imagination;
       it is never more than an argument with the world."

327   Sklar, Robert. "The New Novel, USA: Thomas Pynchon."
       Nation, 25 September 1967, pp. 277-80.

A discussion of the shift in Pynchon's artistic
and intellectual values from V. to Lot 49. Whereas
V. is the first American novel of "collage," Lot 49
is a "radical protest novel," and an "anarchistic
miracle."

328   Stimpson, Catherine R. "Pre-apocalyptic Atavism: Thomas
      Pynchon's Early Fiction," in Mindful Pleasures,
      eds. Levine and Leverenz, pp. 49-67.

      A study of Pynchon's treatment of women in V. and
      Lot 49 especially. In his picture of the decline
      of the west Pynchon treats either the "mothers or
      lovers" by endorsing a sexuality that links itself
      to reproduction.

329   Tanner, Tony. "The American Novelist as Entropologist."
      London Magazine, NS 10 (October, 1970), 5-18.

      REPRINTED:
329a "Everything Running Down," in City of Words. New
      York: Harper and Row, 1971, pp. 141-52.

      The reflective essay on "entropy" and "Manichaean"
      worldviews in contemporary fiction singles out
      Pynchon. A brief discussion of the story "Entropy"
      serves as an introduction.

330   Tanner, Tony. "Patterns and Paranoia or Caries and
      Cabals." Salmagundi, 15 (1971), 78-99.

      REPRINTED:
330a "Caries and Cabals," in City of Words. New York:
      Harper and Row, 1971, pp. 153-80.
330b Mindful Pleasures, eds. Levine and Leverenz, pp.
      49-67.

      A discussion of the "Manichaean terms" dominating
      Pynchon's fiction, most especially the twin axes
      of history/Stencil and modern America/Profane in
      V. Lot 49 is treated with less detail.

331   Trachtenberg, Stanley. "Counterhumor: Comedy in
      Contemporary American Fiction." Georgia Review,
      27/1 (Spring, 1973), 33-48.

      Pynchon briefly mentioned (pp. 45-46).

332   Vesterman, William. "Pynchon's Poetry." Twentieth
      Century Literature, 21/2 (May, 1975), 211-20.

      REPRINTED:
332a Mindful Pleasures, eds. Levine and Leverenz, pp.
      101-12.

In the average of one line of verse per page in Pynchon's novels "the prosody is richest where his subject is most serious or intellectually respectable, because richness of prosody means an increase of comedy in comic songs."

333 Vidal, Gore. "American Plastic: The Matter of Fiction." New York Review of Books, 15 July 1976, pp. 31-39.

A brief discussion of Pynchon (pp. 36-38) in which Mr. Vidal believes that "the prose is pretty bad, full of all the rattle and buzz that were in the air when the author was growing up," and which, in the end, "exhausts patience and energy."

334 Winston, Matthew. "The Quest for Pynchon." Twentieth Century Literature, 21/3 (October, 1975), 278-87.

REPRINTED:
334a Mindful Pleasures, eds. Levine and Leverenz, pp. 251-63.

An attempt to gather "the fragments of his life" and thus provide biographical underpinnings for the novels. Though sketchy and inferential, the facts are interesting, especially those dealing with family history. A new story by Pynchon (see "The Small Rain") was discovered in the process.

335 Young, James D. "The Enigma Variations of Thomas Pynchon." Critique, 10 (1968), 69-77.

A discussion of the "enigmatic" V. and Lot 49, which is "a briefer, more schematic version of V." Pynchon's characterization and naming ("Character as Fiction"), his use of the past ("History as Fiction"), and his use of place ("Geography as Fiction") are then treated.

b. V.

336 Alter, Robert. "The Apocalyptic Temper." Commentary, 41/5 (June, 1966), 61-66.

A reaction to R. W. B. Lewis' Trials of the Word and apocalyptic literature in general. On V.: "the imagined end of all things is in this elaborately ironic presentation ludicrous as well as disturbing."

337 "American Fiction: The Postwar Years, 1934-1965." Book Week, 26 September 1965, pp. 1-3, 5-7, 18, 20, 22, 24-25.

A brief mention of V. (pp. 7, 20, 24).

338   Bergonzi, Bernard. The Situation of the Novel.
      University of Pittsburgh Press, 1970, pp. 96-100,
      passim.

      A discussion of V. as one of the "absurdist" or
      "comic-apocalyptical" school of novels, "a monu-
      ment to the possibilities of dehumanization."

339   Bryant, Jerry. The Open Decision: The Contemporary
      American Novel and Its Intellectual Background.
      New York: Free Press, 1970, pp. 252-57.

      A discussion of V. as an "elaborate examination of
      the relationship between rationality and irration-
      ality, between abstractions and existence."
      Stencil, at the end, is still "pursuing leads,"
      though Profane is one "for whom explanation is
      futile."

340   Davis, Robert Murray. "The Shrinking Garden and the
      New Exits: The Comic-Satiric Novel in the Twentieth
      Century." Kansas Quarterly, 1/3 (Summer, 1969), 5-16.

      A brief note on V., whose protagonist has reader
      empathy "far greater than in most previous works
      in the comic-satiric modes."

341   Feldman, Burton. "Anatomy of Black Humor," in The
      American Novel Since World War II, ed. Marcus Klein.
      Greenwich, Conn.: Fawcett, 1969, pp. 224-28.

      A brief note on V.

342   Golden, Robert E. "Mass Man and Modernism: Violence
      in Pynchon's V." Critique, 14/3 (1972), 5-17.

      In Pynchon's view of the role of mass society, the
      end of individual choice and responsibility is at
      hand. In V. "humanity is something we earn," and
      it is saved from being a "gloomy" novel by its
      humor, "man's best defense before an indifferent
      universe."

343   Greenberg, Alvin. "The Underground Woman: An Excursion
      into the V-ness of Thomas Pyncheon [sic]." Chelsea,
      27 (December, 1969), 58-65.

      A discussion of the hermaphroditic origins of V.,
      the "double-gendered Venus," used by Pynchon to
      discover "the inversion of the creative human
      potential" whose "sterility" we suffer.

344   Hall, James. "The New Pleasures of the Imagination."
      Virginia Quarterly Review, 46/4 (Autumn, 1970), 596-

612.

A discussion of contemporary fantasy, with V.
as a model (pp. 604-12). "Pynchon's fantasy serves
a double purpose as equipment for living" today:
comedy reduces threat and echoes a harmonious past.

345   Harmon, William. "'Anti-Fiction' in American Humor,"
       in The Comic Imagination in American Literature,
       ed. Louis D. Rubin. New Brunswick: Rutgers Univer-
       sity Press, 1973, pp. 381-83.

       A brief discussion of V., especially its "inversion
       and parody of The Scarlet Letter."

346   Hausdorff, Don. "Thomas Pynchon's Multiple Absurdities."
       Wisconsin Studies in Contemporary Literature, 7/3
       (Autumn, 1966), 258-69.

       A study, especially, of Pynchon's use of Henry
       Adams' Autobiography, and the ironies and polari-
       ties which result: the contrast between Virgin
       and Venus, inertia and dynamism, entropy, Stencil's
       third person narrative mode, etc.

347   Henderson, Harry B., III. Versions of the Past: The
       Historical Imagination in American Fiction. New
       York: Oxford University Press, 1974, pp. 278-85.

       A comparison of Barth's The Sot-Weed Factor and
       Pynchon's V. (with reference to Catch-22) in re-
       gard to their use of "roles" and "types." Pynchon,
       however, teaches not "moderation" but "desperation."

348   Hoffman, Frederick J. "The Questing Comedian: Thomas
       Pynchon's V." Critique, 6/3 (Winter, 1963/64),
       174-77.

       An evaluation of V.'s "brilliant profusion" which
       ultimately rejects the novel as a "wearisome joke"
       whose main weakness is that it "makes fun of the
       reason why it makes fun of everything else."

349   Hyman, Stanley Edgar. "The Goddess and the Schlemihl."
       New Leader, 18 March 1963, pp. 22-23.

       REPRINTED:
349a   Standards: A Chronicle of Books for Our Times. New
       York: Horizon, 1966, pp. 138-42.
349b   On Contemporary Literature, ed. Richard Kostelanetz.
       Expanded Edition. New York: Avon, 1969, pp. 506-10.

       A reprint of a favorable review.

350   Koch, Stephen. "Imagination in the Abstract." Antioch
      Review, 24 (Summer, 1964), 253-63.

      A review of V. and Susan Sontag's The Benefactor.
      V., although "sloppy, contorted, bristling with
      immaturity," has "a richness of conception and a
      vividness that can make the abstract imagination,
      even in the throes of its bitter suicide, seem to
      live."

351   Kostelanetz, Richard. "The New American Fiction," in
      New American Arts. New York: Horizon, 1965, pp.
      214-17.

      V. is a "lushly brilliant novel" that is a "vision
      of human life as thoroughly and irrefutably non-
      sensical." Pynchon's knowledge of quantum theory
      "must have influenced his desire to reject causality
      in literature."

352   Larner, Jeremy. "The New Schlemihl." Partisan Review,
      30/2 (Summer, 1963), 273-76.

      V. impresses the reader as the work of a "super-
      scientist," mainly because of its deliberately
      "flattened" prose. In order to realize his potential,
      Pynchon must "throw down the metaphysical apparatus
      and raise something more particular just as high."

353   Lehan, Richard. A Dangerous Crossing. Carbondale:
      Southern Illinois University Press, 1973, pp. 157-62.

      A discussion of V. as "absurd," the novel's two
      plots, and the importance of Vheissu as its
      "embodiment" of "progression."

354   Lewis, R. W. B. Trials of the Word. New Haven: Yale
      University Press, 1965, pp. 228-34.

      A brief discussion of V. as an entropic novel whose
      end "is the world's end."

355   Lhamon, W. T. "Pentecost, Promiscuity, and Pynchon's
      V.: From the Scaffold to the Impulsive." Twentieth
      Century Literature, 21/2 (May, 1975), 163-76.

      REPRINTED:
355a Mindful Pleasures, eds. Levine and Leverenz, pp.
      69-86.

      A discussion of "entropy" and "Pentecostal imagery"
      in V. "Entropy and tongues signify either a state
      of promiscuous equilibrium, or a condition last
      approaching that state."

356   Meixner, John A. "The All-Purpose Quest." Kenyon
       Review, 25/4 (Autumn, 1963), 729-35.

       A review of V. and several other novels in which
       the general reaction is unfavorable: "The best I
       can contrive at the moment to say is that V. may
       be Pynchon's The Voyage Out. But in comparison
       Woolf was fortunate."

357   Patteson, Richard. "What Stencil Knew: Structure and
       Certitude in Pynchon's V." Critique, 16/2 (1974),
       30-44.

       One of V.'s major themes is the "ultimate limita-
       tions of knowledge," and "an expression" of its
       very structure as well. Each of the chapters in
       which V is sought is narrated in a different way --
       an attempt to discover new ways of knowing that
       is ultimately found inadequate.

358   Richardson, Robert O. "The Absurd Animate in Thomas
       Pynchon's V.: A Novel." Studies in the Twentieth
       Century, 9 (Spring, 1972), 35-58.

       A long study of the "passive, inert and inanimate"
       characters who "counterbalance" and "suggest an
       alternative to the chaos, cruelty and destruction"
       in the novel. Benny, especially, Rachel, Esther,
       Paola, McClintic Sphere and Fausto are discussed.

359   Richter, D. H. Fable's End: Completeness and Closure
       in Rhetorical Fiction. University of Chicago Press,
       1974, pp. 101-35.

       In a chapter entitled "The Failure of Completeness"
       Prof. Richter studies Pynchon's inability "to
       produce a work that moves us as a coherent whole"
       in V. Although "magnificent and instructive,"
       Pynchon's "metaphors remain cold conceits; the
       novel is itself inanimate."

360   Schulz, Max F. Black Humor Fiction of the Sixties:
       A Pluralistic Definition of Man and His World.
       Athens, Ohio: Ohio University Press, 1973, pp. 61-
       64, 77-82, passim.

       A discussion of the "inmost revelation" in Pynchon's
       novels and the various parodies he engages the
       reader in, especially in V.

361   Schulz, Max F. "Pop, Op, and Black Humor: The Aesthetics
       of Anxiety." College English, 30/3 (December, 1968),
       230-41.

A brief discussion of V.'s depiction of the "col-
lective" and "passive" hero of our century, and
its "hallucination" of the "logic of history."

362   Slatoff, Walter. "Thomas Pynchon." Epoch, 12/4
      (Spring, 1963), 255-57.

      A review of V. which is entirely affirmative,
      announcing that Pynchon "has the vitality, intelli-
      gence, skill, and magic to become one of the major
      writers of our time."

363   Wasson, Richard. "Notes on a New Sensibility."
      Partisan Review, 36/3 (1969), 460-77.

      A discussion of V. (pp. 470-75) along with several
      other books. This "modern satiric novel," trying
      "to forge new myths," rejects the notion that
      mythology "can be used to order the chaos of
      history."

364   Widmer, Kingsley. The Literary Rebel. Carbondale:
      Southern Illinois University Press, 1965, pp. 155,
      238.

      A discussion of Pynchon as an example of "ornate
      bohemian literature."

365   Ziolkowski, Theodore. "The Telltale Teeth: Psycho-
      dontia to Sociodontia." PMLA, 91/1 (January, 1976),
      9-22.

      Although the discussion centers mainly on the works
      of Günter Grass, Dostoievsky, Mann, Koestler and
      others, there is a brief reflection on the Eigen-
      value episode in V.

                  c. The Crying of Lot 49

366   Abernathy, Peter. "Entropy in Pynchon's The Crying
      of Lot 49." Critique, 14/3 (1972), 18-33.

      The novel depicts America as a "series of closed
      systems," which are explicated here, and thus
      reminiscent of the work of contemporaries like
      Heller in Catch-22. The ending is inconclusive,
      both "ambiguous and apocalyptic."

367   Berthoff, Warner. Fictions and Events: Essays in
      Criticism and Literary History. New York: Dutton,
      1971, p. 113.

      A brief reference to the "final vision" of Lot 49
      as indicative of the "subservience that takes the

form of pretending" in contemporary fiction.

368   Davis, Robert M. "Parody, Paranoia, and the Dead
End of Language in The Crying of Lot 49." Genre,
5/4 (December, 1972), 367-77.

Lot 49 is a "post-realistic novel" that embodies
"the death of wonder and the total entropy of
energy and commumication." "If Pynchon is not able
to make the leap of faith, he can only retreat and
thus repeat himself -- a kind of literary entropy."

369   Kirby, David K. "Two Modern Versions of the Quest."
Southern Humanities Review, 5/4 (Fall, 1971), 387-
95.

A study of two fictional ("Quest") heroines, Oedipa
in Lot 49 and the governess in James' The Turn of
the Screw. The novel poses epistemological
as well as moral problems, and is, indeed, "about
the limits of human knowledge."

370   Kolodny, Annette and Daniel J. Peters. "Pynchon's
The Crying of Lot 49: The Novel as Subversive
Experience." Modern Fiction Studies, 19/1 (1973),
79-87.

The novel forces us "to embrace the reality of
ambiguity, uncertainty, and barely-perceived in-
tuition" of America. It is a "kind of journey to
the underworld," and "an indictment of America"
as well as an exploration of the "latent possibilities" in America and its language.

371   Leland, John P. "Pynchon's Linguistic Demon: The
Crying of Lot 49." Critique, 16/2 (1974), 45-53.

Entropy infects the entire novel, its preoccupations
and techniques. Lot 49 is "anti-mimetic" -- "its
words deny easy access to things, its symbols fail
to symbolize, its allegorical correspondences
crumble within a circular structure of words."

372   Lyons, Thomas R. and Allan D. Franklin. "Thomas
Pynchon's 'Classic' Presentation of the Second
Law of Thermodynamics." Bulletin of the Rocky
Mountain Language Association, 27 (1973), 195-204.

An extensive discussion of Pynchon's use of this
particular scientific metaphor and fact, especially
in Lot 49.

373   Mangel, Anne. "Maxwell's Demon, Entropy, Information:
The Crying of Lot 49." TriQuarterly, 20 (Winter, 1971),

194-208.

REPRINTED:
373a   Mindful Pleasures, eds. Levine and Leverenz, pp.
        87-100.

A discussion of three scientific concepts in Lot
49: thermodynamics and Maxwell's demon, entropy,
and information theory. Pynchon, thus, radically
separates himself from traditional novelists and
allies himself with "contemporary artists working
in other media who incorporate scientific ideas
and seek randomness in art."

374   May, John R. Toward a New Earth: Apocalypse in the
       American Novel. Notre Dame University Press, 1972,
       pp. 180-91.

A discussion of the "mood of unfolding revelation"
in Lot 49, its central motif. "In the symbolism
of the apocalypse, The Crying of Lot 49 converts
the moment of warning prior to disaster into the
impersonal category of anticipated revelation."

375   Mendelson, Edward. "The Sacred, The Profane, and
       The Crying of Lot 49," in Individual and Community:
       Variations on a Theme in American Fiction, eds.
       Kenneth H. Baldwin and David K. Kirby. Durham:
       Duke University Press, 1975, pp. 182-222.

A long analysis of Lot 49, especially in contrast
to V. "Almost all the incidents in V. enact a decline in available energy," whereas in Lot 49 "a
hidden order reinforces Pynchon's world without
energy, adds to the world's complexity, and demands
not acquiescence but conscious choice."

376   Poirier, Richard. "Embattled Underground." New York
       Times Book Review, 1 May 1966, p. 5.

REPRINTED:
376a   The Performing Self. New York: Oxford University
        Press, 1971, pp. 23-26.

One of the original affirmative reviews.

377   Puetz, Manfred. "Thomas Pynchon's The Crying of Lot
       49: The World Is a Tristero System." Mosaic, 7/4
       (1974), 125-37.

Whether the conspiracy Oedipa seeks exists or not,
her "ambition to detect order in history," though
commendable, becomes "a neurotic obsession" which
reveals "man's final lapse into a state of paranoid

delusions."

378 Wagner, Linda W. "A Note on Oedipa the Roadrunner."
     Journal of Narrative Technique, 4 (1974), 155-61.

     Lot 49 creates the "speed" that dominates our
     culture. Oedipa is presented sympathetically, for
     she endures, in the face of "impossible situations,"
     as a "persevering innocent" in a "paranoid and
     divisive culture."

               d. Gravity's Rainbow

379 Friedman, Allen J. and Manfred Puetz. "Science as
     Metaphor: Thomas Pynchon and Gravity's Rainbow."
     Contemporary Literature, 15 (Summer, 1974), 345-59.

     Central to the novel's metaphor and characters is
     "thermodynamics." In the abundance of Pynchon's
     universe there are two types: those who believe in
     deterministic conspiracy (paranoia) or in complete
     randomness (anti-paranoia).

380 Fussell, Paul. The Great War and Modern Memory. New
     York: Oxford University Press, 1975, pp. 328-34.

     A discussion of the General Pudding episode in
     which Pynchon seems to be proposing that "the
     Great War" was "the ultimate origin of the insane
     contemporary scene." The analysis of the "Mistress
     of the Night" episode in Gravity's Rainbow is con-
     vincing.

381 Gilbert-Rolfe, Jeremy and John Johnston. "Gravity's
     Rainbow and the Spiral Jetty." October, 1/1 (Spring,
     1976), 65-85 and 1/2 (Summer, 1976), 71-90.

     A very technical comparison of Pynchon's novel and
     Robert Smithson's architectural design. Some points
     of similarity are: entropy, Freud's "metonymy of
     Eros and Thanatos," European and American impulses,
     and the relationship of modernism to the epic.

382 Kaufman, Marjorie. "Brunnhilde Among the Chemists,"
     in Mindful Pleasures, eds. Levine and Leverenz,
     pp. 197-227.

     A discussion of the female characters in Gravity's
     Rainbow. The seven women treated seem to reveal that
     Pynchon is demonstrating more than "the views of
     radical feminism," but "compassion and love for
     victor and victim alike" as well.

383 Kihss, Peter. "Pulitzer Jurors Dismayed on Pynchon."

New York Times, 8 May 1974, p. 38.

The reasons why Pynchon was ultimately denied the
prize for Gravity's Rainbow.

384   LeClair, Thomas. "Death and Black Humor." Critique,
      17/1 (1975), 5-40.

      A brief discussion (pp. 25-28) of Gravity's Rainbow
      and the theme of death, "the efficient cause of
      behavior" for Pynchon, even though it is located
      in "the tissues of history itself."

385   Leverenz, David. "On Trying to Read Gravity's Rain-
      bow," in Mindful Pleasures, eds. Levine and Leverenz,
      pp. 229-49.

      The novel is a "dualistic melodrama" that results
      in "an inextricable jumble of sympathies and
      quarrels." Although the themes might be objected
      to, "the most powerfully aching language for natural
      description in our literature" is worthy of "aston-
      ished praise."

386   Leverenz, David. "Point Counterpoint." Partisan Review,
      42/4 (1975), 643.

      A letter in response to Neil Schmitz' article on
      pp. 112-25. Mr. Schmitz replies, pp. 643-44.

387   Levine, George. "V-2." Partisan Review, 40/3 (Fall,
      1973), 517-29.

      A long review of Gravity's Rainbow in which Pynchon
      is described as "the most important American novel-
      ist now writing." Forms, plots, energies, surfaces,
      styles, assimilation of cultures, allusions and
      myths are discussed.

388   Lhamon, W. T. "The Most Irresponsible Bastard." New
      Republic, 14 April 1973, pp. 24-28.

      A long review of Gravity's Rainbow, "the massive,
      mind-blowing, stomach-turning, monstrously comic
      new milestone in fiction." Its genius, he concludes,
      will "depress all competition."

389   Mendelson, Edward. "Gravity's Encyclopedia," in
      Mindful Pleasures, eds. Levine and Leverenz, pp. 161-
      95.

      An elaborate essay on Gravity's Rainbow as "en-
      cyclopedic narrative," the "prophecy and satire"
      that a national culture produces when it becomes

fully conscious of itself. After a careful textual discussion, Prof. Mendelson concludes that this may be the first "international" encyclopedic narrative ever written.

390 Mendelson, Edward. "Pynchon's Gravity." Yale Review, 62 (Summer, 1973), 624-31.

A long review and discussion of Weber's concept of "charisma" as central to Gravity's Rainbow. Both Slothrop, the protagonist, and the Rocket, the central symbol, struggle against the "routinization of charisma."

391 Ozier, Lance W. "Antipointsman/Antimexico: Some Mathematical Imagery in Gravity's Rainbow." Critique, 16/2 (1974), 73-90.

An analysis of mathematical allusions, which "significantly strengthen the thematic structure" of the novel. An example: the contrast between Roger Mexico (lover, accepter of life's indeterminacy) and Edward Pointsman (manipulative behaviorist), both scientists.

392 Ozier, Lance W. "The Calculus of Transformation: More Mathematical Imagery in Gravity's Rainbow. Twentieth Century Literature, 21/2 (May, 1975), 193-210.

Mathematical references seem "to connect and clarify" some of the difficulties of the novel. Fundamental calculus "and the idea of transformation they suggest constitutes an affirmation that is true to Pynchon's view of the world."

393 Poirier, Richard. "Rocket Power." Saturday Review of the Arts, March, 1973, pp. 59-64.

A long review of Gravity's Rainbow which centers on Pynchon's role in contemporary letters: "More than any living writer, he has caught the inward movements of our time in outward manifestations of art and technology."

394 Rosenbaum, Jonathan. "One Man's Meat is Another Man's Poisson." Village Voice, 29 March 1973, pp. 24, 26.

A generally favorable review with one reservation: will Gravity's Rainbow "seem as dated in 40 years as Dos Passos' USA appears today?"

395 Sanders, Scott. "Pynchon's Paranoid History." Twentieth Century Literature, 21/2 (May, 1975), 177-92.

86

REPRINTED:
395a   Mindful Pleasures, eds. Levine and Leverenz, pp.
        139-59.

        The "conspiratorial view of history" that "struc-
        tures Pynchon's fiction" is discussed, especially
        the "theology" from which "God has been withdrawn."
        Prof. Sanders concludes by positing four objections
        against Pynchon's view of man and history.

396   Schmitz, Neil. "Describing the Demon: The Appeal of
        Thomas Pynchon." Partisan Review, 42/1 (1975), 112-
        25.

        A discussion of Pynchon's history as "theatre,"
        especially in Gravity's Rainbow. His "Manichean"
        world-view and obsession with "obscene history"
        make his work "anti-establishment," offering "the
        ethics of the desperado."

397   Schwarzback, F. S. "Pynchon's Gravity." New Review,
        3/27 (June, 1976), 39-43.

        A general introduction to Pynchon's fiction, espe-
        cially Gravity's Rainbow to the British audience,
        including a survey of his themes and preoccupations.

398   Simmon, Scott. "A Character Index: Gravity's Rainbow."
        Critique, 16/2 (1974), 68-72.

        A list of page references for every named character
        in the novel.

399   Simmon, Scott. "Gravity's Rainbow Described." Critique,
        16/2 (1974), 54-67.

        An exploration of the novel's theme: "an historical
        and cultural synthesis of Western culture and fan-
        tasies." Also discussed: characterizations in
        Freudian terms, dualistic and cinematic structure,
        and five interrelated plots.

400   Thorburn, David. "A Dissent on Pynchon." Commentary,
        56/3 (September, 1973), 68-70.

        A dissonant voice speaking out against the "Pynchon
        cult," and especially Gravity's Rainbow, "a deeply
        confused and finally unpersuasive work," mainly
        because of its unconvincing characters.

VI
Dissertations

See Section V for published dissertations or
extracts from dissertations.

i. Hawkes

401   Camara, George C. "War and the Literary Extremist:
       The American War Novel, 1945-1970." Diss. Mass.
       1974.

402   Eichel, Seymour. "Myth, Ritual and Symbol in the
       Novels of John Hawkes." Diss. N.Y.U. 1973.

403   Emmett, Paul. "John Hawkes: An Analysis of His Work
       and His Place in Contemporary Literature." Diss.
       Chicago 1976.

404   Fitzgerald, Ellen. "World War II in the American
       Novel: Hawkes, Heller, Kosinski, and Vonnegut."
       Diss. Notre Dame 1974.

405   Frost, Helen L. P. "A Legacy of Violence: John
       Hawkes' Vision of Culture." Diss. Rochester 1970.

406   Glass, Terence L. "Myths, Dreams, and Reality: Cycles
       of Experience in the Novels of John Hawkes." Diss.
       Ohio State 1974.

407   Golden, Robert E. "Violence and Art in Postwar Ameri-
       can Literature: A Study of O'Connor, Kosinski,
       Hawkes and Pynchon." Diss. Rochester 1972.

408   Green, James L. "Nightmare and Dream in John Hawkes'
       Novels." Diss. Nevada 1972.

409   Heath, William R. "John Hawkes: A Critical Study."
       Diss. Case Western Reserve 1971.

410   Heineman, Alan Charles. "Amusing Creations Out of
       Poisonous Smoke: The Novels of John Hawkes."
       Diss. Brandeis 1974.

411   Johnson, Joseph J. "The Novels of John Hawkes and
       Julien Gracq: A Comparison." Diss. Vanderbilt 1970.

412   Leana, Frank C. "The Power of Language in the Novels

of John Hawkes." Diss. Rochester 1974.

413   LeClair, Thomas. "Final Words: Death and Comedy in
       the Fiction of Donleavy, Hawkes, Barth, Vonnegut,
       and Percy." Diss. Duke 1973.

414   Meese, George. "The Use of Rhetorical Criticism to
       Determine Value in Imaginative Prose Literature:
       Value in the Novels of John Hawkes." Diss. Chicago
       1976.

415   Nelson, Paula K. "The Function of Figures of Speech
       in Selected Anti-Realist Novels." Diss. N.Y.U. 1972.

416   Norwood, Vera L. H. "Whatever Happened to Natty
       Bumppo? John Hawkes and the American Tradition."
       Diss. New Mexico 1974.

417   Olderman, Raymond Michael. "Beyond the Waste Land:
       A Study of the American Novel in the Nineteen-
       Sixties." Diss. Indiana 1969.

418   Scott, Henry E., Jr. "'The Terrifying Similarity':
       The Themes and Techniques of John Hawkes." Diss.
       Wisconsin 1968.

419   Slotnick, Linda. "The Minotaur Within: Varieties of
       Narrative Distortion and Reader Implication in the
       Works of Franz Kafka, John Hawkes, Vladimir Nabo-
       kov and Alain Robbe-Grillet." Diss. Stanford 1971.

420   Smith, Marcus Ayers Joseph, Jr. "The Art and Influ-
       ence of Nathanael West." Diss. Wisconsin 1965.

421   Tajuddin, Mohammad. "The Tragicomic Novel: Camus,
       Malamud, Hawkes, Bellow." Diss. Indiana 1968.

422   Weinstein, Sharon R. "Comedy and Nightmare: The
       Fiction of John Hawkes, Kurt Vonnegut, Jr., Jerzy
       Kosinski and Ralph Ellison." Diss. Utah 1971.

423   Yskamp, Claire E. "Character and Voice: First Person
       Narrators in Tom Jones, Wuthering Heights, and
       Second Skin." Diss. Brandeis 1972.

ii. Heller

424   Camara, George C. "War and the Literary Extremist:
       The American War Novel, 1945-1970." Diss. Mass.
       1974.

425   Finkel, Jan M. "Techniques of Portraying the Gro-

tesque Character in Selected Writings of Nathaniel
Hawthorne, Sherwood Anderson and Joseph Heller."
Diss. Indiana 1974.

426 Fitzgerald, Ellen. "World War II in the American
Novel: Hawkes, Heller, Kosinski, and Vonnegut."
Diss. Notre Dame 1974.

427 Fort, Deborah C. "Contrast Epic: A Study of Joseph
Heller's Catch-22, Günter Grass' The Tin Drum,
John Barth's The Sot-Weed Factor and Vladimir
Nabokov's Pale Fire." Diss. Maryland 1974.

428 Frank, Michael. "Rhetoric, Theme and Consciousness
in Catch-22: An Essay in Critical Reading." Diss.
Cornell 1972.

429 Harris, Charles B. "Contemporary American Novelists
of the Absurd." Diss. Southern Illinois 1971.

430 Haverman, Carol S. P. "The Fool as Mentor in Modern
American Parables of Entrapment: Ken Kesey's One
Flew Over The Cuckoo's Nest, Joseph Heller's
Catch-22, and Ralph Ellison's Invisible Man."
Diss. Rice 1971.

431 Hearron, William T. "New Approaches in the Post-Modern
American Novel: Joseph Heller, Kurt Vonnegut, and
Richard Brautigan." Diss. S.U.N.Y. Buffalo 1973.

432 Janoff, Bruce L. "Beyond Satire: Black Humor in the
Novels of John Barth and Joseph Heller." Diss.
Ohio 1972.

433 Kennard, Jean Elizabeth. "Towards A Novel of the
Absurd: A Study of the Relationship Between the
Concept of the Absurd as Defined in the Works of
Sartre and Camus and Ideas and Form in the Fiction
of John Barth, Samuel Beckett, Nigel Dennis, Joseph
Heller, and James Purdy." Diss. California at
Berkeley 1968.

434 Kilgo, James P. "Five American Novels of World War II:
A Critical Study." Diss. Tulane 1972.

435 Kochanek, Patricia S. "In Pursuit of Proteus: A
Piagetian Approach to the Structure of the Grotesque
in American Fiction in the Fifties." Diss. Penn
State 1973.

436 Luttrell, William. "Tragic and Comic Modes in Twentieth Century American Literature: William Styron
and Joseph Heller." Diss. Bowling Green 1969.

437   Olderman, Raymond Michael. "Beyond the Waste Land:
        A Study of the American Novel in the Nineteen-
        Sixties." Diss. Indiana 1969.

438   Reilly, Charles. "The Ancient Roots of Modern Satiric
        Fiction: An Analysis of 'Petronian' and 'Apuleian'
        Elements in the Novels of John Barth, J. P. Donleavy,
        Joseph Heller, James Joyce, and Vladimir Nabokov."
        Diss. Delaware 1974.

439   Rice, Joseph Allen. "Flash of Darkness: Black Humor
        in the Contemporary American Novel." Diss. Florida
        State 1967.

440   Ritter, Jesse Paul, Jr. "Fearful Comedy: The Fiction
        of Joseph Heller, Günter Grass, and the Social
        Surrealist Genre." Diss. Arkansas 1967.

441   Robinson, David E. "Unaccomodated Man: The Estranged
        World in Contemporary American Fiction." Diss.
        Duke 1972.

442   Smith, Marcus Ayers Joseph, Jr. "The Art and Influence
        of Nathanael West." Diss. Wisconsin 1965.

443   Stark, Howard J. "Catch-22: The Anatomy of a Novel."
        Diss. New Mexico 1968.

444   Valencia, Willa Ferree. "The Picaresque Tradition
        in the Contemporary English and American Novel."
        Diss. Illinois 1968.

                        iii. Pynchon

445   Golden, Robert E. "Violence and Art in Postwar Ameri-
        can Literature: A Study of O'Connor, Kosinski,
        Hawkes and Pynchon." Diss. Rochester 1972.

446   Grant, J. K. "The Embroidered Mantle: Order and the
        Individual in the Fiction of Thomas Pynchon."
        Diss. Virginia 1976.

447   Harris, Charles B. "Contemporary American Novelists
        of the Absurd." Diss. Southern Illinois 1971.

448   Krafft, John M. "Historical Imagination in the
        Novels of Thomas Pynchon." Diss. Buffalo 1976.

449   Olderman, Raymond Michael. "Beyond the Waste Land:
        A Study of the American Novel in the Nineteen-
        Sixties." Diss. Indiana 1969.

450   Plates, William M. "Metamorphosis: An Examination of
      Communications and Community in Barth, Beckett and
      Pynchon." Diss. Illinois 1974.

451   Ritter, Jesse Paul, Jr. "Fearful Comedy: The Fiction
      of Joseph Heller, Gunter Grass, and the Social
      Surrealist Genre." Diss. Arkansas 1967.

452   Robinson, David E. "Unaccomodated Man: The Estranged
      World in Contemporary American Fiction." Diss.
      Duke 1972.

453   Sperry, Joseph P. "Henry Adams and Thomas Pynchon:
      The Entropic Movements of Self, Society and Truth."
      Diss. Ohio State 1975.

454   Wazeka, Robert Thomas. "The Solitary Escape in
      Recent American Literature." Diss. Colorado 1972.

VII
Bibliographies

i. Hawkes

455 Adelman, Irving and Rita Dworkin. The Contemporary
     Novel: A Checklist of Critical Literature on the
     British and American Novel Since 1945. Metuchen,
     N. J.: Scarecrow, 1972, pp. 250-52.

456 Bryer, Jackson. "Bibliography," Critique, 6/2 (Fall,
     1963), 89-94.

     The first bibliography on Hawkes: an excellent
     compilation of reviews on The Cannibal, The Beetle
     Leg, The Goose on the Grave and The Lime Twig.
     Little criticism had been published by 1963.

457 Busch, Frederick. "Bibliographical Note," in John
     Hawkes: A Guide To His Fictions, pp. 183-86.

     A prose commentary on works by and about Hawkes
     through the late sixties. A good guide.

458 Greiner, Donald J. "Selected Checklist of John
     Hawkes," in Comic Terror, pp. 249-53.

     A fine selective bibliography.

459 Kuehl, John. "Bibliography," in Sweetness and Blood,
     pp. 191-95.

     A fine introductory bibliography through the early
     seventies.

460 Olds, Marshall. Unpublished, but frequently cited.

461 Plung, Daniel. "John Hawkes: A Selected Bibliography:
     1943-1975." Critique, 17/3 (1976), 55-63.

     A good bibliography, especially strong in gathering
     reviews for all of the Hawkes volumes.

ii. Heller

462 Adelman, Irving and Rita Dworkin. The Contemporary

Novel. Metuchen, N. J.: Scarecrow, pp. 253-54.

463   Ethridge, James M., Barbara Kopala and Carolyn Riley.
       Contemporary Authors: A Bio-bibliographical Guide
       to Current Authors and Their Works. Detroit: Gale,
       1968, vii/viii, pp. 237-38.

464   Gerstenberger, Donna and George Hendrick. The Ameri-
       can Novel: A Checklist of Twentieth Century Criti-
       cism on Novels Written Since 1789. Chicago: Swallow,
       1970, II, 163-64.

465   Harte, Barbara and Carolyn Riley. Contemporary Authors:
       Bio-Bibliographies of Selected Writers of Today With
       Critical and Personal Sidelights. Detroit: Gale, 1969,
       pp. 142-43.

466   Kiley, Frederick and Walter McDonald. "Bibliographical
       Note," in A Catch-22 Casebook, pp. 391-96.

       A fine, inclusive bibliography which supplements
       the selections in the casebook and which is rela-
       tively exhaustive through 1973.

467   Leary, Lewis. Articles on American Literature, 1950-
       1967. Durham, N. C.: Duke University Press, 1970,
       pp. 261-62.

468   Nagel, James. "Suggested Readings for Further Study,"
       in Critical Essays on Catch-22, pp. 175-79.

       A selective but good bibliography.

469   Scotto, Robert M. "A Checklist of Critical Works on
       Catch-22," "Representative Reviews," and "The
       Printing History of Catch-22," in A Critical
       Edition of Catch-22, pp. 560-62.

       Up to date as of 1972.

470   Weixlmann, Joseph. "A Bibliography of Joseph Heller's
       Catch-22." Bulletin of Bibliography, 31/1 (January/
       March, 1974), 32-37.

       A comprehensive bibliography through early 1973,
       especially noteworthy for its citation of thirty-
       eight reviews of the novel and selections from book-
       length studies of literature which refer, however
       briefly, to Catch-22.

iii. Pynchon

471   Adleman, Irving and Rita Dworkin. The Contemporary
       Novel. Metuchen, N. J.: Scarecrow, 1972, pp. 438-39.

472   Ethridge, James M., et. al. Contemporary Authors.
       Detroit: Gale, 1968, xix-xx, 352-54.

473   Gerstenberger, Donna and George Hendrick. The Ameri-
       can Novel. Chicago: Swallow, 1970, II, p. 297.

474   Harte, Barbara and Carolyn Riley. Contemporary
       Authors. Detroit: Gale, 1969, pp. 223-24.

475   Herzberg, Bruce. "Selected Articles on Thomas Pynchon:
       An Annotated Bibliography." Twentieth Century
       Literature, 21/2 (May, 1975), 221-25.

       A selective but representative bibliography, care-
       fully annotated.

       REPRINTED:
475a   Levine and Leverenz, eds. Mindful Pleasures, pp.
       265-69.

       A much fuller bibliography, strong on reviews of
       the novels, but not annotated.

476   Leary, Lewis. Articles on American Literature. Durham,
       N. C.: Duke University Press, 1970, p. 463.

477   Weixlmann, Joseph N. "Thomas Pynchon: A Bibliography."
       Critique, 14/3 (1972), 34-43.

       A fine checklist which is complete through 1971,
       and has an especially impressive list of the
       reviews of V. and The Crying of Lot 49.